EXCELLENT ENGINEERING

Rob Beattie

illustrated by Sam Peet

QEB

Quarto is the authority on a wide range of topics.

Quarto educates, entertains and enriches the lives of our readers—enthusiasts and lovers of hands-on living.

www.quartoknows.com

© 2019 Quarto Publishing plc

First published in 2019 by QEB Publishing
an imprint of The Quarto Group.
6 Orchard Road
Suite 100
Lake Forest, CA 92630
T: +1 949 380 7510
F: +1 949 380 7575
www.QuartoKnows.com

A CIP record for this book is available from the Library of Congress.

ISBN: 978-1-78603-368-0

Manufactured in Shenzhen, China HH102018

9 8 7 6 5 4 3 2 1

Editor: Nancy Dickmann
Project Editor: Emily Pither
Editorial Director: Laura Knowles
Art Director: Susi Martin
Publisher: Maxime Boucknooghe
Production: Nikki Ingram
Consultant: Pete Robinson

CONTENTS

4   Introduction

6   Key Equipment

8   Paper Pillars

10   Newton's Cradle

14   The Simple Circuit

16   Crafty Catapult

18   Tower of Triangles

20   Hi-tech Hand

22   The Paper Loudspeaker

26   Geodesic Dome

28   Jumping Marbles

30   Homemade Nightlight

32   Engineer's Arm

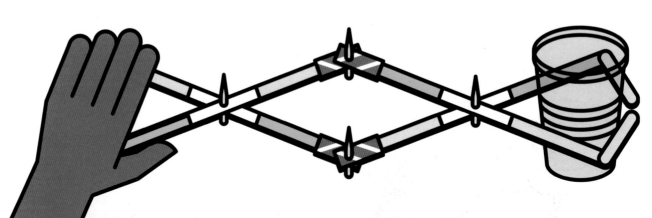

34 The Bouncing Bridge

38 Weather Vane

40 Magnetic Spinner

42 Double Cup Flyer

44 Marble Roller Coaster

46 Clothesline Flyer

50 Electric Spinner

52 Paper Popper

54 Robot Artist

56 The Bottle Rocket

58 The Marble Maze

62 Supersonic Straw

64 The Dancing Robot

66 The Bottle Sub

68 The Hanging Arch

70 Rubber Band Boat

74 The Electric Light Show

76 Balloon Racer

78 The Trembling Tower

80 The Bottle Blaster

82 Big Dipper

86 The Wave Machine

88 Smartphone Boombox

90 The Simple Machines

94 Glossary

96 Index

INTRODUCTION

Welcome to Excellent Engineering! This book will show you that the everyday objects lying around the house— things that you don't think twice about—are actually amazing. In the right hands (that means your hands!) these items can do astounding things.

Exploring Engineering

Engineering is about experimenting, trying things out and solving problems. The projects in this book are perfect for putting your engineering skills to the test. Using the handy step-by-step instructions, you can try out lots of engineering techniques as well as building cool stuff that you can keep and use again. There's a wide range of projects: some are straightforward and some are more challenging and will take longer.

Below each page number, you will find one of three symbols. This lets you know which engineering category the project belongs in.

 Structural—building stuff that's designed to stay up on its own, support other things (such as a bridge), or resist outside forces (like an earthquake).

 Mechanical—making things that move.

 Electrical—creating things that use electricity, electronics, and magnetism.

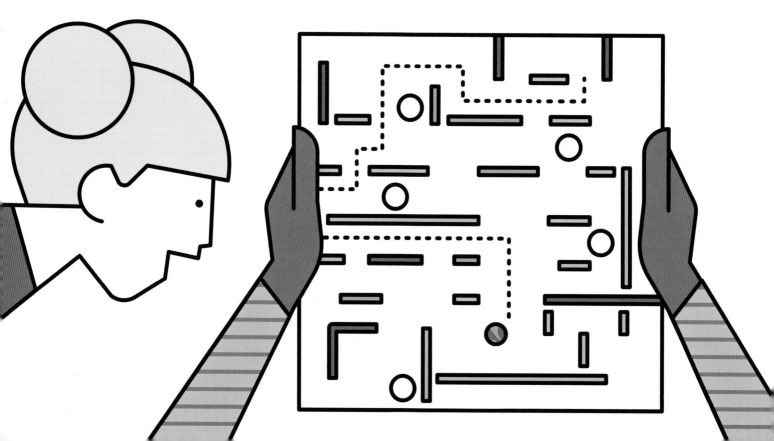

Safety first

We've used a traffic-light system to label each project, showing whether or not you need adult supervision. The "traffic lights" are on the page numbers. Here's how it works:

- Green—no adults required! You're on your own, but don't sweat it: you got this. DO check with an adult before you start experimenting, though!

- Amber—some of the steps require an adult to supervise or actually carry them out. They usually involve knives or fire or a substance that needs handling with care.

- Red—you must have an adult on hand because some or all of the steps require help or supervision. You're still in charge, but they should do the dangerous stuff...

Like all engineers, make sure you follow any health and safety advice for the equipment and materials you use.

Inside engine...

Look ou... that acc... project. T... the fascinating science behind the project and help you to understand exactly what's going on.

In the real world

These boxes look at the ways that the project can be applied in real life.

Take it further
These boxes will show you how to take the experiment a step further and develop your scientific skills.

KEY EQUIPMENT

Here's a guide to the main equipment you will need to complete the projects in this book. Where possible we've used the kind of everyday items you'll have cluttering up your house anyway—push pins, rubber bands, cardstock, cardboard boxes, string, paper cups, and so on. However, there are a few specialized bits of equipment that you'll need. You can get most of these from a DIY or craft shop, or online.

Batteries

Some projects use a 3 volt, round lithium battery (which looks like a silver coin) or a 9 volt battery, which is rectangular and has two terminals at one end.

Copper wire

Projects that use electricity usually require copper wire. The uncoated type is best, but it can be harder to find than the enameled kind.

Craft sticks

You can also use popsicle sticks but you'd have to buy (and eat) an awful lot of ice cream (which perhaps is not such a bad thing!).

Copper tape

This useful tape is sticky on one side but, unlike regular tape, it can conduct electricity!

Craft knife

These knives are better at scoring and cutting different materials than an ordinary knife, but that's because they are razor-sharp. Get an adult to help with the cutting when you're using one of these.

Crocodile clips

These useful metal clips can be used to make a temporary electrical connection.

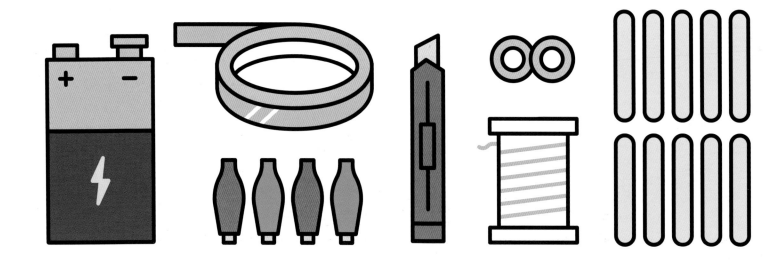

Duct tape

Sometimes confusingly called "duck" tape, this is strong, very sticky tape coated in polythene.

Hexbug

These inexpensive, tiny robots have a built-in motor that's perfect for making other things vibrate.

Hot glue gun

You can use other types of glue, but a glue gun is flat out the best, most fun, and most effective way to do the gluing you need in this book. But there is a very important clue in the name! This gun gets HOT and so does the glue, so you need to use it with adult supervision and always switch it off when you're finished.

LEDs

These tiny lights each have two "legs"—one positive and one negative. They light up when electricity is passed through them.

Masking tape

Tape with a paper feel which attaches to most surfaces. It's easy to remove and doesn't leave any marks.

Neodymium magnets

These work like "normal" magnets but are much more powerful and better suited for engineering work. But be warned: they're so stong they can give little fingers a nasty nip and you'll find they attract all sorts of metal objects when you're least expecting it, so be careful. Make sure to keep them away from phones, computers, and other electronic gadgets!

Pipe insulation

You'll need a few lengths of this plastic foam tubing, designed to go around water and heating pipes in your house.

Protractor

Getting the right angle can be important, and a protractor will help you measure angles correctly.

Ring magnets

These are large round magnets with a hole in the middle. They are sometimes called "donut magnets"—it's easy to see why!

That's it! Have fun, but remember that if you're unsure about the safety of any items used in this book, check with an adult first.

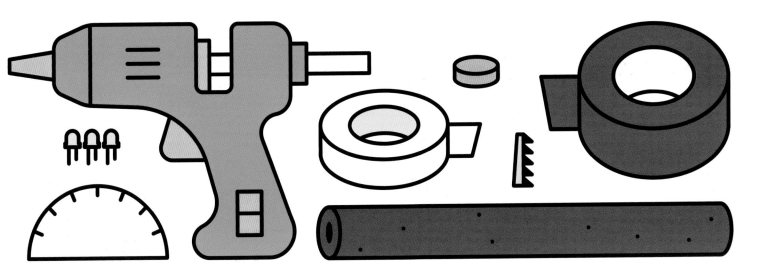

PAPER PILLARS

How many books do you think four sheets of ordinary paper can support? The answer may surprise you...

You will need
- **4 sheets of printer paper**
- **Clear tape**
- **Several books**
- **Flat surface**

1.5 IN

1 Roll one of the sheets of paper into a tube, starting with one of the shorter ends, and tape the end into place. Your tube should be about 1.5 inches (4 cm) in diameter.

2 Repeat step 1 with the other three sheets of paper, so you have four identical tubes.

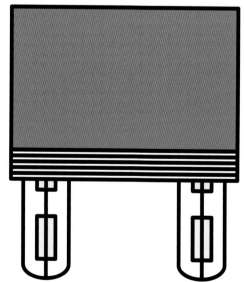

3 Stand the tubes up on a flat surface. They should be placed in a rectangle arrangement, just smaller than the size of your largest book.

4 Carefully balance a book on top of your paper pillars. If it falls down, stand the pillars back up and try again.

5 Once your pillars and book are stable, carefully add another book.

6 If your pillars are still standing, keep adding books, one at a time. How many books can you balance on your pillars before the whole thing collapses?

Take it further Try out some other pillar arrangements to test whether they are as strong and stable as four arranged in a square or rectangle. You could try a single pillar, positioned in the middle of a book, or two pillars in a line. Then place two pillars at opposite corners and see if that improves your results.

Inside the engineering

A flat sheet of paper is not very strong, but when you roll it into a tube—or pillar—it becomes a rigid structure. This makes it much stronger, and good at bearing loads. When you arrange four pillars—one at each corner—the weight of the books is distributed between all four pillars, so no one pillar has to support too much weight. This setup gives you an ideal combination of strength and balance.

NEWTON'S CRADLE

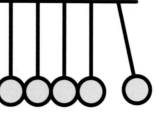

6 IN

You may have seen a Newton's Cradle before, but did you know that it hides a secret prized by engineers?

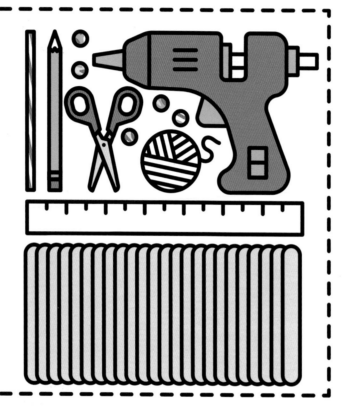

You will need
- 24 craft sticks
- Plastic straw
- 5 marbles
- String
- Scissors
- Ruler
- Hot glue gun
- Pen/Pencil

1 Cut five identical pieces of string, each 6 inches (15 cm) long.

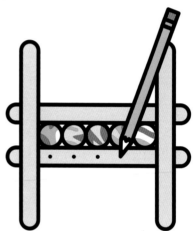

2 Lay out two craft sticks parallel with each other, then slide the marbles in between them. Use two more sticks at either end to keep the marbles in place. Mark where the middle of each marble is on one of the sticks.

3 Set the marbles to one side and line up the marked craft stick next to another one. Use the ruler to mark lines across both.

4 Using a glue gun, carefully stick the five pieces of string on top of the lines you just made on one of the craft sticks. Try to line up the ends of the strings with the edge of the stick.

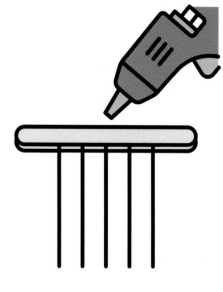

5 Glue a second craft stick onto the top, making a "sandwich" with the strings inside.

6 Cut five small pieces of straw. Each one should be about half or two-thirds the width of a marble.

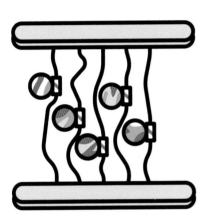

7 Glue each piece onto a marble.

8 Thread each of the marbles onto one of the five pieces of string.

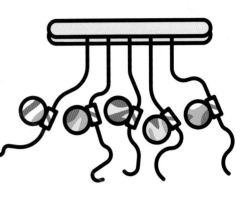

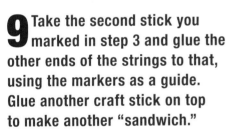

9 Take the second stick you marked in step 3 and glue the other ends of the strings to that, using the markers as a guide. Glue another craft stick on top to make another "sandwich."

10 Now it's time to make a frame. Add a blob of glue to each end of the top stick, and attach a craft stick to both.

11 Flip the whole thing over and glue a stick along the bottom, to connect the two sticks you added in step 10.

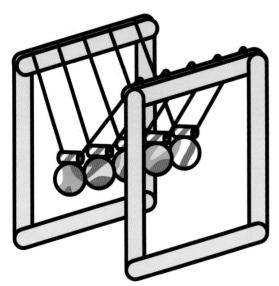

12 Repeat steps 10 and 11 on the other craft stick "sandwich."

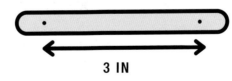

3 IN

13 Take another craft stick, measure out a 3 inch (7.5 cm) length in the middle, and mark it.

14 Using this stick as a template, mark nine more sticks in the same way. Cut them so that you have ten identical 3 inch (7.5 cm) lengths and line them up.

3 IN

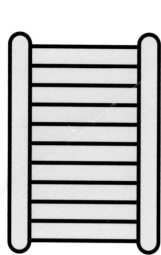

15 Use the ruler to hold the sticks in position while you glue a whole craft stick lengthways on top.

16 Glue a second stick down the other side. This will form the base of your cradle.

17 When all the glue has dried, apply glue down one side of the base and attach it to one of the sides of the cradle. Hold it together until the glue sets.

3 IN

18 Apply glue to the other side of the base and attach it to the other side of the cradle in the same way. When the glue is dry, stand the cradle upright.

19 Cut two more 3 inch (7.5 cm) lengths of craft stick.

20 Glue these to the front and back of the cradle frame at the top. They will help keep it stable.

21 Make sure that the marbles line up and are at the same height—you can adjust the strings if you need to. Lift the marble at one end and let it swing back and hit the other four marbles. The three in the middle should hardly move, but the one at the far end will bounce away and then come back.

Take it further Try lifting two marbles at the same time, letting them go and watching what happens to the marbles at the other end. Also, if you can find five matching steel balls to make your cradle, these will work better than marbles. They are heavier and will have more momentum.

Inside the engineering

The cradle demonstrates something called the conservation of momentum and the conservation of energy. When the moving ball hits the four stationary balls, it transfers a force through them. To conserve energy and momentum, only one ball at the opposite end moves. In theory, if there were a thousand marbles in the cradle, the force would be transferred through the line and momentum would be transferred from the first marble to the thousandth marble. The cradle only works with balls that do not absorb much energy. Even marbles and ball bearings absorb a little energy in each collision, which makes the cradle eventually stop swinging.

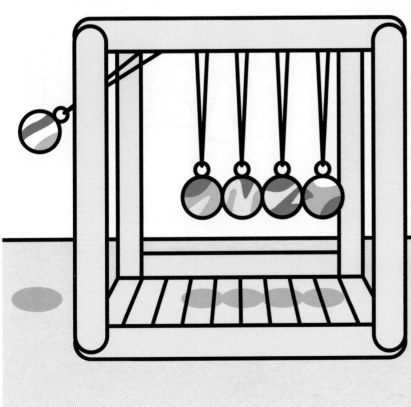

THE SIMPLE CIRCUIT

Here's a bright idea! Let's build a simple circuit using some tape, a battery, and an LED.

You will need
- **Sheet of printer-size cardstock**
- **Marker or pencil**
- **Ruler**
- **LED light**
- **Copper foil tape (with conductive adhesive)**
- **Clear tape**
- **3 volt round lithium battery**
- **Scissors**

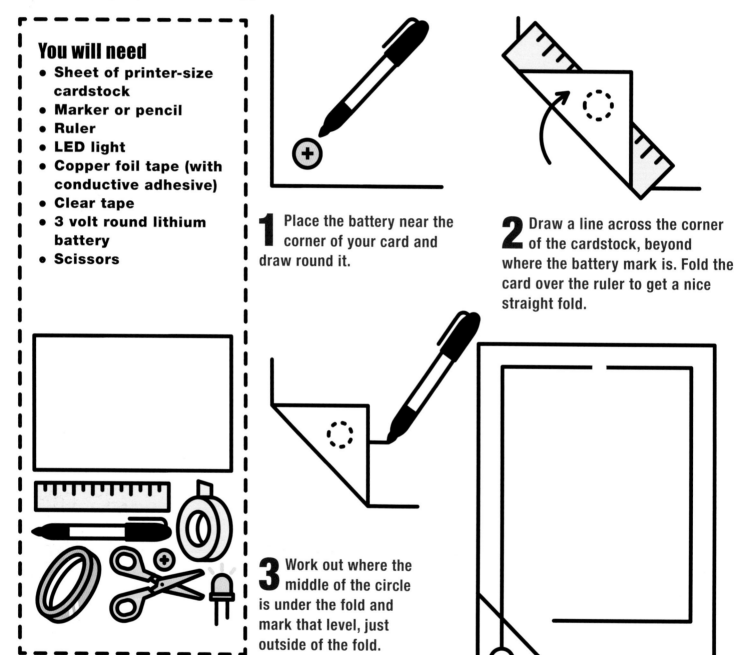

1 Place the battery near the corner of your card and draw round it.

2 Draw a line across the corner of the cardstock, beyond where the battery mark is. Fold the card over the ruler to get a nice straight fold.

3 Work out where the middle of the circle is under the fold and mark that level, just outside of the fold.

4 Draw a rectangle on the cardstock. Make sure the bottom edge joins up with the mark you made in step 3, but stops short of completing the rectangle. You should also leave a small gap in the middle of the top side.

Inside the engineering

Electricity can flow through copper. The negative side of the battery touches the copper tape that extends to the negative side of the light. When you fold the corner over, the positive side of the battery touches the copper tape that extends to the positive side of the light. This completes the circuit.

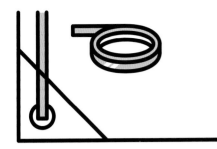

5 Peel the end of the backing off the copper tape. Stick the tape onto the cardstock, down the left hand side, from the middle of the circle, to about 2 inches (5 cm) from the top of the cardstock. Cut the tape.

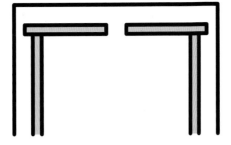

6 Cut and stick tape along the top of the rectangle, making sure to leave a little gap in the middle.

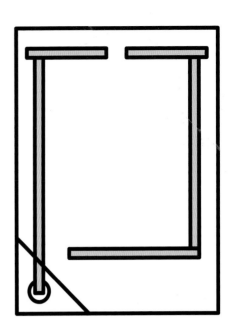

7 Follow the rest of the line, sticking tape down as you go. When you're done you'll have a small gap at the top and a bigger one in the bottom left corner.

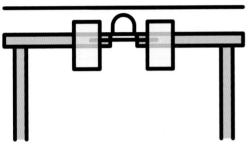

8 Take your LED light and bend the legs out. Use clear tape to tape the legs of the LED onto the copper tape, closing the gap at the top of the cardstock. The long leg should be on the left and the shorter leg on the right.

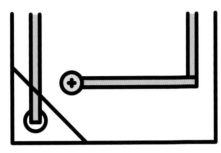

9 The positive side of the battery has a "+" sign. Place it down on the cardstock with the positive side facing up. It should sit at the end of the copper tape along the bottom, where it stops just short of reaching the left-hand edge.

10 Fold the corner of the cardstock over so the circle you drew in step 1 touches the positive side of the battery. The LED will light up!

Troubleshooting

If your light doesn't come on, try flipping the battery over. Still nothing? LED lights are pretty easy to break, so try using a new one. Still no good? Make sure you're using a battery rated to at least 3 volts.

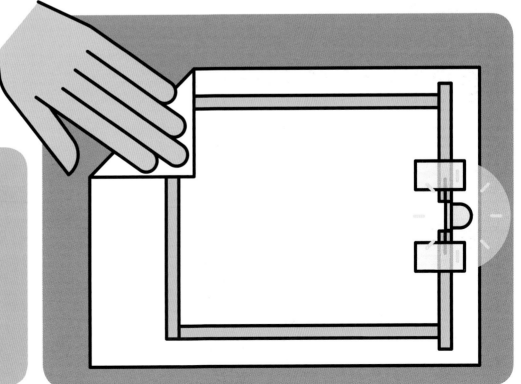

CRAFTY CATAPULT

Armies have been using catapults to propel objects through the air for thousands of years. Now it's your turn.

You will need
- 12 wooden craft sticks
- 3 medium-sized rubber bands
- Hot glue gun
- Small plastic bottle top
- Scrap paper

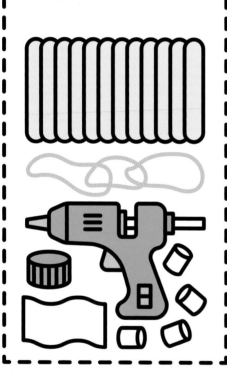

In the real world

The idea behind a catapult is that it can throw a missile farther and faster than a person can throw the same object; it can also throw much heavier things than you can. The catapult was important in battle because it could hurl missiles over high walls—or even through them.

1 Take 10 craft sticks and gather them together to make a stack.

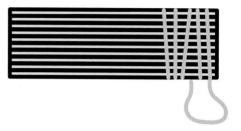

2 Wrap a rubber band around one end of the stack to hold the sticks together. Keep wrapping until the band is tight and the stack is secure.

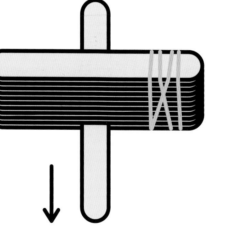

3 Take one of the remaining craft sticks and slide it in between the bottom two craft sticks in your stack.

4 Take a second rubber band and wrap it around the other end of the stack to secure the craft stick added in step 3.

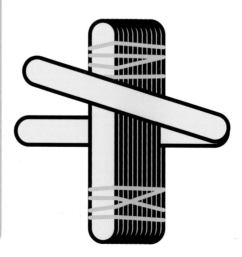

5 Take the final craft stick and place it on top of the stack. Hold it against the bottom stick to make a "V" shape.

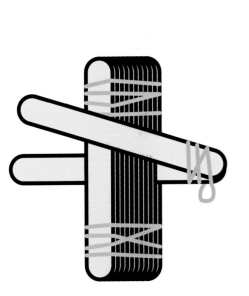

6 Wrap the final rubber band around the ends of the top and bottom sticks to hold them in place.

7 Use the glue gun to put a good-sized dollop of glue on the end of the top stick.

8 Stick the bottle top to the end of the top craft stick to form the cup of your catapult.

9 Let the glue dry for a couple of minutes, then roll up a scrap of paper to make a "missile." Drop it into the cup of the catapult, then, holding the other end to keep everything steady, gently pull back and release to fire!

Take it further If you make several catapults you can have a competition with your friends to see which one shoots the farthest. Do it outside and mark the distances with chalk. Experiment with different "missiles"—mini marshmallows make good ones—but be careful and make sure you avoid using anything hard.

Inside the engineering

When you pull back the stick, you transfer energy to the catapult. This energy is stored in the catapult until you let go—when it transfers to kinetic energy in the paper, which is powerful enough to throw the paper through the air.

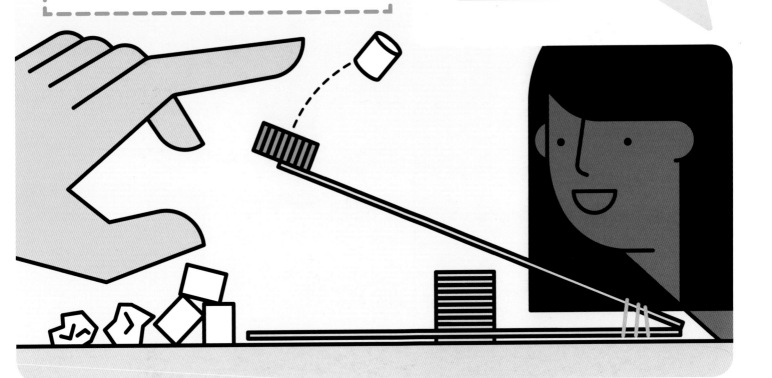

TOWER OF TRIANGLES

How can you make cardstock strong enough to build with? By making it into triangles!

You will need

- **Several sheets of strong colored printer-size cardstock**
- **Ruler**
- **Pen or pencil**
- **Clear tape**
- **Scissors**
- **Craft knife**

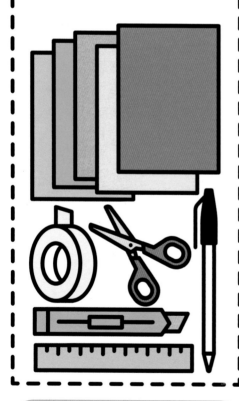

In the real world

The Egyptian pyramids have four sides, and each one is an equilateral triangle. They must be strong, as some have been standing for more than 4,000 years!

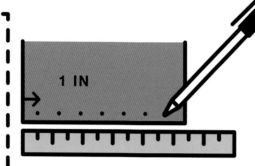

1 Measure along the bottom of a sheet of cardstock, making a mark every 1 inch (2.5 cm). Do the same along the top of the cardstock.

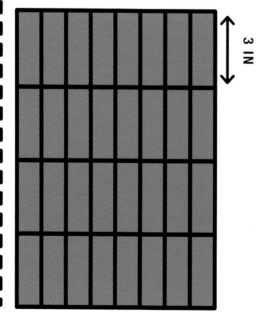

3 Measure along the long sides of the cardstock, making a mark every 3 inches (7.5 cm). Draw lines to connect these marks and you'll end up with a sheet of rectangles which measure 1 by 3 inches (2.5 by 7.5 cm).

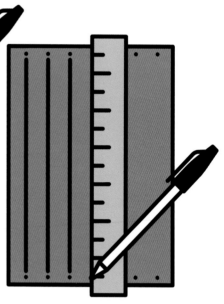

2 Use the ruler to draw lines across the cardstock, connecting the marks at each end.

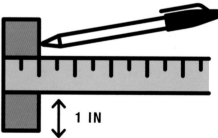

4 Cut out the rectangles and use your ruler to make lines dividing each into three equal sections, each about 1 inch (2.5 cm) long.

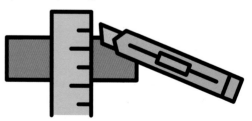

5 Take the craft knife and ask an adult to score very lightly down the two marked lines.

6 Fold the sides up and push the two open ends together to form a triangle. Secure it with a bit of clear tape.

7 Keep scoring, folding, and taping until you have a big pile of identical triangles. You could recruit a friend to help you!

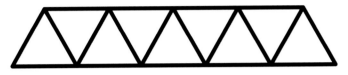

8 Now it's time to start building! Line up five triangles, then put four more upside down on top of them.

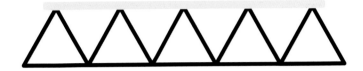

9 Cut a long strip of cardstock 1 inch (2.5 cm) wide and lay it on top of your line of triangles.

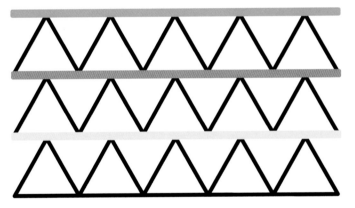

10 Add more rows of triangles on top, then another strip of cardstock, then even more triangles. How high can you go?

11 Test the stability of your structure by taking triangles away from the bottom couple of rows and putting them on the top.

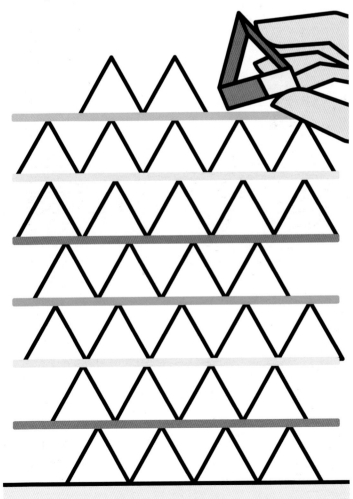

Inside the engineering

Triangles are the strongest and most stable shape you can build with. Our triangles are "equilateral," which means that all three sides are the same length. This makes them even stronger. The triangle gets its strength because it's difficult to distort its shape—in fact, it'll break before that happens. If you used squares, pushing down on the top would cause them to "hinge" sideways and your structure would fail.

HI-TECH HAND

Have you always been fascinated by how robots work? If so, you'll jump at the chance to make a simple robot hand that actually moves!

You will need
- Sheet of heavy printer-size cardstock
- Ruler
- Scissors
- Pencil
- Two large straws
- Masking tape
- String
- Hot glue gun

1 Use your ruler to draw a 4 by 4 inch (10 by 10 cm) square on the cardstock, then cut it out.

2 On the remaining cardstock, use the ruler to measure out five identical columns. Each one should be 3/4 inches (2 cm) wide and 3 inches (7.5 cm) long. These will be the "fingers."

3 Divide each column into three 1 inch (2.5 cm) sections. Cut out the 15 pieces.

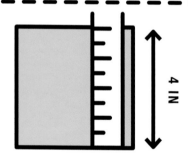

4 Lay out the pieces to form a hand shape.

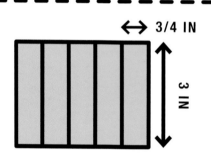

5 Cut 20 lengths of straw. They don't have to be exactly the same size, but each one must be less than 1 inch (2.5 cm) long.

6 Glue three pieces of straw onto three of the small cardstock rectangles.

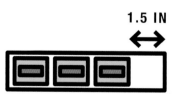

7 Cut a length of masking tape about 1.5 inches (4 cm) longer than the "finger." Stick the three sections onto the tape.

Take it further Get your friends to join in by putting each one in charge of one of the fingers while you operate the thumb. See how many gestures you can make with your hi-tech hand.

8 Place the "finger" under the hand and press down so the extra tape sticks to the "back." Glue another bit of straw on the "palm" underneath the finger.

Inside the engineering

By dividing the fingers and thumb into three "joints" we're able to make the hand move realistically by using the string to create a very simple pulley system. Pulleys do lots of clever things—here the pulleys (the bits of string running through the straws) let you pull in one direction and have the fingers move in a different direction.

9 Cut a piece of string about 6 inches (15 cm) long and thread it through the straws. Wrap a bit of string over the end of the finger and secure it with a small piece of tape.

10 Repeat steps 6-9 for the other three fingers and thumb to complete your hand.

11 You may have to hold the "palm" down with your finger, but when you pull on the different strings you can make the hi-tech hand move like a real robot hand!

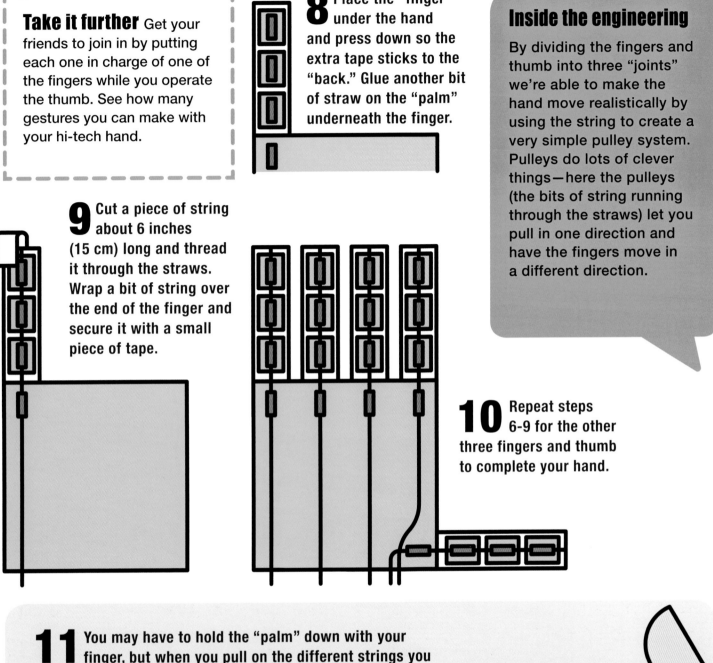

THE PAPER LOUDSPEAKER

Loudspeakers are complicated things, right?
You couldn't possibly make one, right? Well, there's
nothing an engineer loves more than a challenge...

You will need
- **Paper plate**
- **Plastic or styrofoam bowl**
- **3 round neodymium magnets**
- **Clear tape**
- **Ruler**
- **Pen or marker**
- **Scissors**
- **Craft knife**
- **Sheet of printer paper**
- **About 3 feet (almost 1 m) of enameled copper wire, less than 1mm thick**
- **Hot glue gun**
- **Lighter**
- **Stereo system**

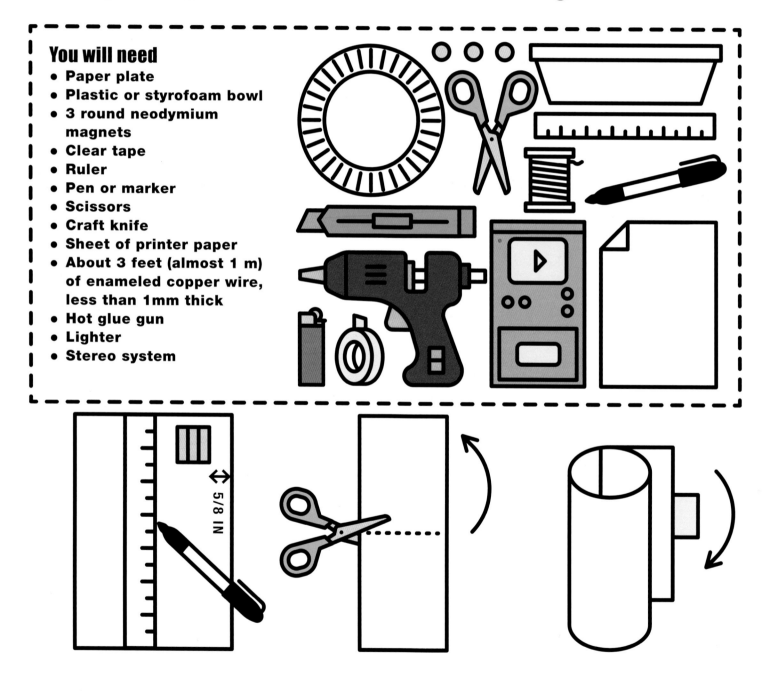

5/8 IN

1 Stack your magnets to make a pillar, then lay them sideways on the paper. Draw a line down the paper, leaving about 5/8 inch (1.5 cm) on either side of the magnets.

2 Cut out the strip of paper, then fold it in half and cut it into two equal strips.

3 Take the first piece of paper and roll it around your magnets. Use clear tape to stick the paper in place, forming a tube around the magnets.

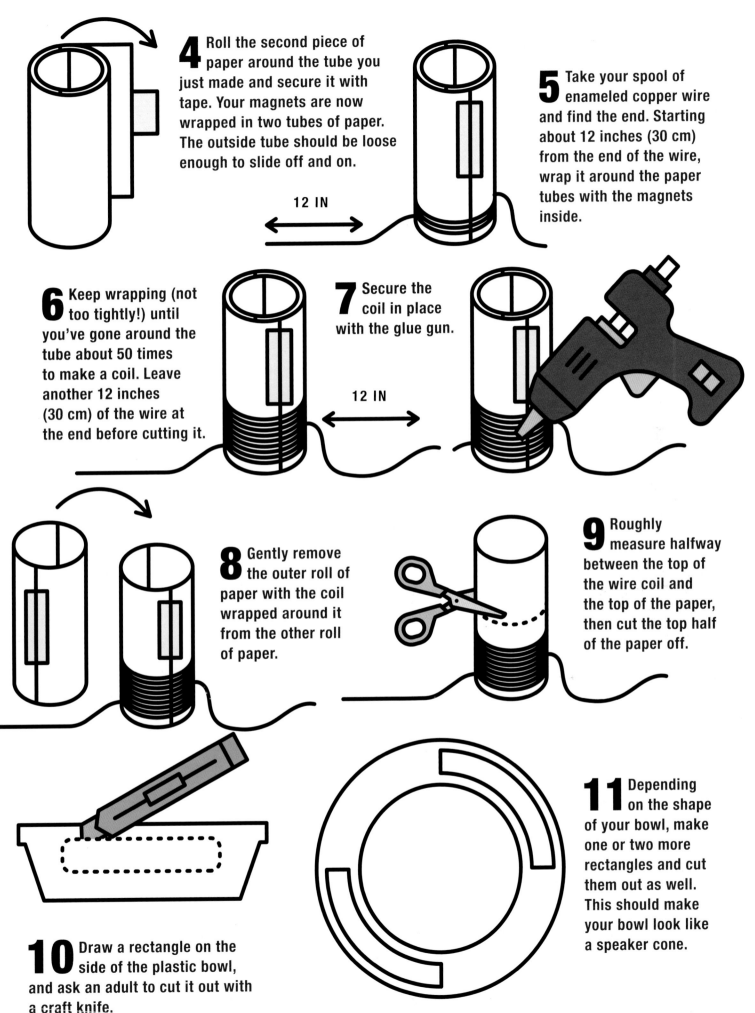

4 Roll the second piece of paper around the tube you just made and secure it with tape. Your magnets are now wrapped in two tubes of paper. The outside tube should be loose enough to slide off and on.

12 IN

5 Take your spool of enameled copper wire and find the end. Starting about 12 inches (30 cm) from the end of the wire, wrap it around the paper tubes with the magnets inside.

6 Keep wrapping (not too tightly!) until you've gone around the tube about 50 times to make a coil. Leave another 12 inches (30 cm) of the wire at the end before cutting it.

7 Secure the coil in place with the glue gun.

12 IN

8 Gently remove the outer roll of paper with the coil wrapped around it from the other roll of paper.

9 Roughly measure halfway between the top of the wire coil and the top of the paper, then cut the top half of the paper off.

10 Draw a rectangle on the side of the plastic bowl, and ask an adult to cut it out with a craft knife.

11 Depending on the shape of your bowl, make one or two more rectangles and cut them out as well. This should make your bowl look like a speaker cone.

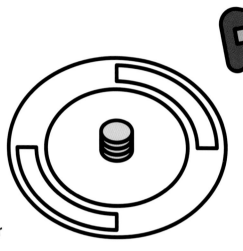

12 Pull the inner roll of paper off the magnets—you don't need it any more. Put a couple of dabs of glue onto one end of the magnet pillar.

13 Stick the magnets to the middle of the bowl.

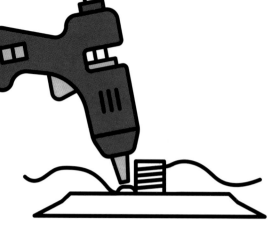

14 Take the roll of paper with the wire coil wrapped around it and glue it to the bottom of the paper plate, right in the middle.

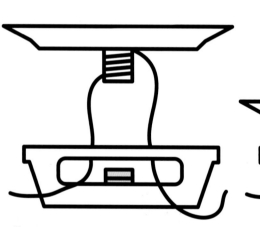

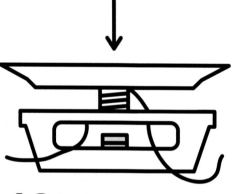

15 When that's dry, flip the plate over and take the two loose ends of wire. Thread them through one of the rectangular holes in the bowl.

16 Gently position the paper roll above the magnets and slide it on.

17 Glue the plate to the top of the bowl. If you push the plate in the center, it should go down and then bounce up again when you let go.

18 It's time for your adult assistant again! They need to burn both ends of the wire with a lighter, to remove the coating. You should just be left with copper.

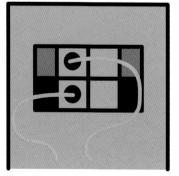

19 Ask your adult to unplug any speakers that are attached to the stereo system. Then they should connect the wires of your paper loudspeaker where the normal speaker wires plug in.

Take it further If you want to make your speaker look more high tech, try painting it—this won't make it louder but will make it look cooler!

Inside the engineering

The signal from the stereo is a kind of alternating current, which changes direction all the time—a bit like mains electricity. When it flows through the coil of wire it keeps getting attracted to the magnet and then repelled again. This happens really quickly. The coil of wire vibrates, making the plate pulse. The paper roll then amplifies (makes louder) these vibrations so that you can actually hear the sound.

20 Pop in a CD, press play, and listen through your very own speaker, made using the same principles that make "real" speakers work!

GEODESIC DOME

The futuristic geodesic dome is one of the most stable and solid structures ever designed. Here's how to make your own.

You will need

- **At least 35 large plastic straws, 9.5 inches (24 cm) long**
- **Paper fasteners**
- **Wooden skewer**
- **Ruler**
- **Scissors**

1 Make a mark 5 inches (13 cm) from one end of a straw and cut it. Do the same for four more straws, so you end up with five straws 5 inches (13 cm) long and five straws 4.5 inches (11 cm) long.

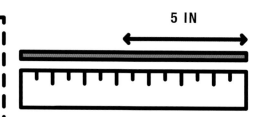

5 IN

2 Use the skewer to poke a hole through one of the straws, almost at the end. Poke another hole at the other end of the straw, then repeat for the other nine straws.

3 Push a paper fastener through two of your 5 inch (13 cm) straws and fold open its "wings" to lock it in position.

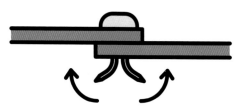

4 Continue linking the 5 inch (13 cm) straws until all five are joined together to make a pentagon.

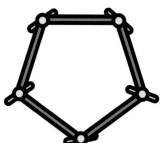

In the real world

To see a geodesic dome in action, check out the Eden Project in Cornwall, where you'll find eight giant interlinked transparent domes. Spaceship Earth at Walt Disney World, Florida, is an example of a geodesic sphere (two domes "stuck" together).

5 Flip the pentagon over and close one of the fasteners. Push one of the short straws onto it and then open the wings again to secure it. Do this at each joint.

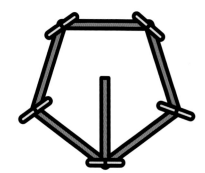

6 Use another paper fastener to secure all five of the shorter straws. Your pentagon is finished!

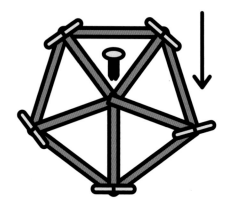

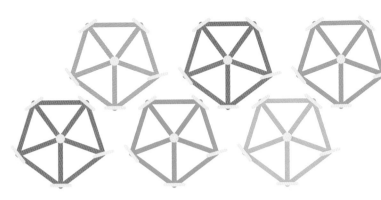

7 Repeat steps 1–6 until you have six identical pentagons.

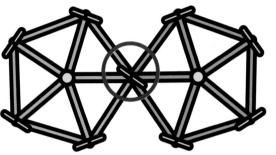

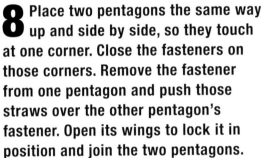

8 Place two pentagons the same way up and side by side, so they touch at one corner. Close the fasteners on those corners. Remove the fastener from one pentagon and push those straws over the other pentagon's fastener. Open its wings to lock it in position and join the two pentagons.

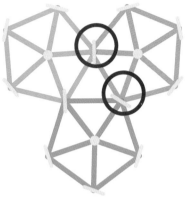

9 Join a third pentagon to the other two in the same way.

10 Then add two more, so the pentagon in the center has another pentagon at each corner. Add the final pentagon, securing it to the one in the middle and the ones on either side.

11 With five pentagons joined to the central one, you should be able to see the shape of the dome clearly.

12 Cut five more 5 inch (13 cm) straws and use them to connect the five gaps at the bottom of the dome. You now have an incredibly strong structure!

Inside the engineering

As explained on pages 18–19, triangles are very stable shapes. This is mainly because they're so hard to bend out of shape— especially when they're surrounded by other triangles. The compression on any joint is balanced by the tension along the opposite side.

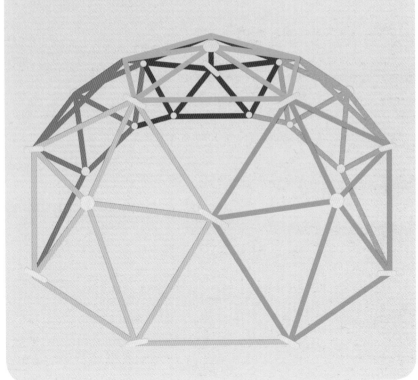

JUMPING MARBLES

A paper toy with a mind of its own, powered by a couple of marbles? Who wouldn't like to have one of those?

You will need
- Sheet of printer paper
- Pencil
- Ruler
- Scissors
- Two marbles
- Large coin (or other round object about 1 inch (2.5 cm) across)
- Clear tape
- A sloped surface

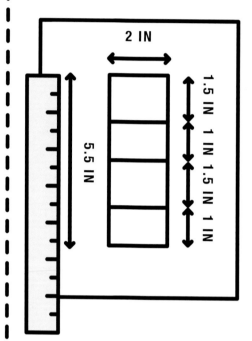

1 In the middle of the paper, draw a column that's 2 inches (5 cm) across and 5.5 inches (14 cm) high. Divide it into four sections so the first is 1.5 inches (4 cm), the second is 1 inch (2.5 cm), the third is 1.5 inches (4 cm), and the last is 1 inch (2.5 cm).

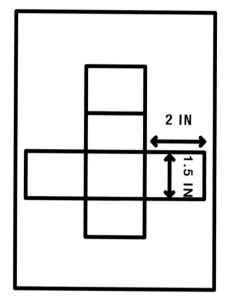

2 Draw a pair of rectangular "wings" on either side of the third section. Each wing should be 2 inches (5 cm) across and 1.5 inches (4 cm) high.

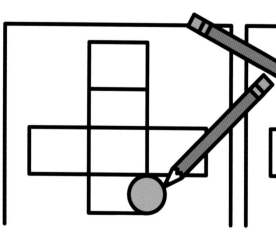

3 Place the coin so the center sits on the outside edge of the bottom 1 inch (2.5 cm) section. Draw around the right hand side with the pencil to end up with a half-circle.

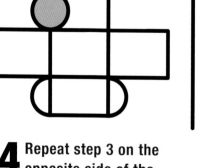

4 Repeat step 3 on the opposite side of the bottom section, then draw half-circles on each side of the other 1 inch (2.5 cm) section.

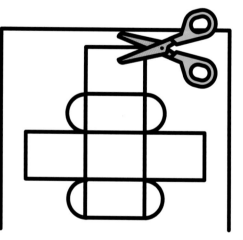

5 Check your measurements, then carefully cut out the entire shape.

6 Fold the shape along the lines – but don't fold in the half-circles.

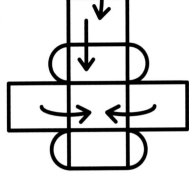

7 Make a 'roof' by bringing the top and bottom edges together and securing them with tape.

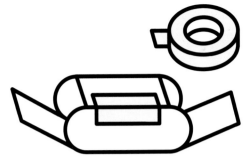

8 Bend one of the rectangular "wings" into a curve and tape it into place to create a rounded front. Tape the top and the sides for extra security.

9 Drop the two marbles into the shape.

10 Bend the other rectangular "wing" and tape it into place.

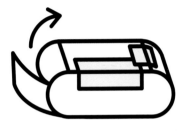

11 Place the toy at the top of a slope and let it go. It will jerk its way to the bottom without any help from you!

Take it further Try decorating your toy by painting it black, with yellow lightning bolts on the side. Or you could add a set of googly eyes at either end!

WOW!

Inside the engineering

The toy jerks its way to the bottom because of a combination of gravity and the slope. Gravity is the force that pulls objects toward Earth's center and makes the marbles roll down the slope on the inside of the toy. They hit the lower end and their inertia pulls the back end of the toy up and over. Then the whole motion starts again! With each turn the toy picks up speed.

HOMEMADE NIGHTLIGHT

Have you ever wondered how an incandescent light bulb works? You can find out by making your own.

You will need
- Small clear plastic bottle
- Piece of mains electrical wire with stripped ends
- Four miniature crocodile clips
- 9 volt alkali battery
- Plastic cap with wires for 9 volt battery
- Modeling clay or adhesive putty
- Craft knife
- Scissors
- Mechanical pencil

1 Take the first crocodile clip and pull the metal part out of the plastic sleeve.

2 Push the end of one of the stripped wires through the plastic sleeve in its place.

3 Push the end of the wire through the little hole in the metal clip and lay the rest between the two prongs on the back.

4 Pinch the two prongs together to secure the wire, then push the plastic sleeve back over the metal clip.

5 Repeat steps 1–4 for the other three clips. You should end up with a wire that has two clips at either end.

6 Ask an adult to cut off the bottom of the plastic bottle with the craft knife. You should end up with a little plastic dome about 4 inches (10 cm) high.

4 IN

Inside the engineering

The pencil "lead" isn't made of lead at all— it's graphite. When you complete the circuit by touching the final two clips to the battery, the electricity runs through the wires. When it reaches the graphite, it heats it to a high temperature. That's why the graphite gives off smoke and then glows, like the filament in a light bulb.

7 Cut a small "V" shape in the bottom of the dome for the cable to go through.

8 Roll out the modeling clay into a rough circle, the same size as the bottom of the bottle.

9 Stand two of the crocodile clips upright by pressing them into the clay. Make sure their openings line up.

10 Take a length of lead out of the pencil. Opening the clips one at a time, clip the lead into position between them.

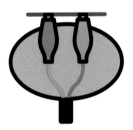

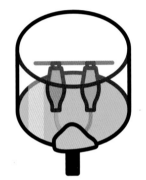

11 Place the plastic dome over the two clips, pushing it down into the modeling clay to make a seal. Then cover any gaps where the wires go in with another blob of clay.

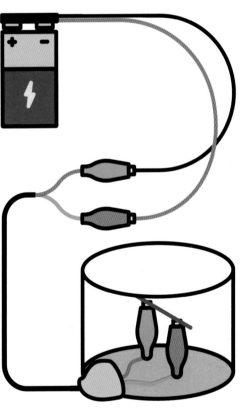

12 Pop the plastic cap onto the battery, then attach the two remaining clips to the two wires coming off the battery cap.

13 After a second or two, the pencil lead will begin to smoke and then glow red. For best results, try it in the dark!

The pencil lead gets to a temperature of several hundred degrees when it is glowing. DO NOT TOUCH!

ENGINEER'S ARM

If you've ever wished that your arms were just that little bit longer, then you're going to love this "Engineer's Arm."

You will need
- **Nine craft sticks**
- **1 large drinking straw**
- **2 wooden skewers**
- **Masking tape**
- **Scissors**
- **Hot glue gun**

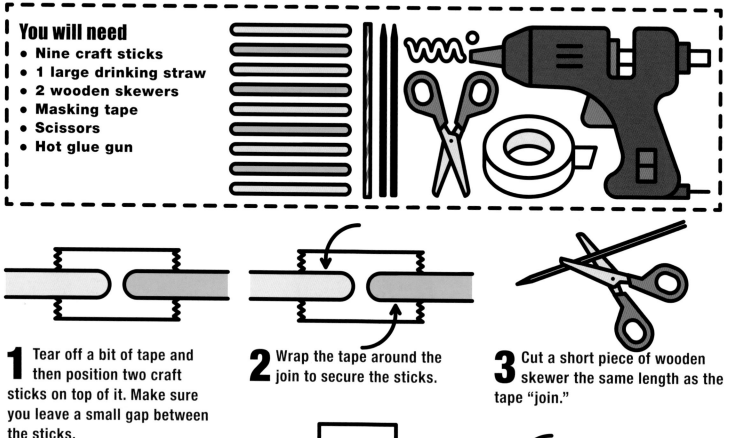

1 Tear off a bit of tape and then position two craft sticks on top of it. Make sure you leave a small gap between the sticks.

2 Wrap the tape around the join to secure the sticks.

3 Cut a short piece of wooden skewer the same length as the tape "join."

4 Then, tear a second piece of tape the same length, lay sticks on top of it, and position the skewer as shown.

5 Wrap the second piece of tape around the sticks and skewer to hold everything in place.

In the real world

You'll often see arms like this behind round mirrors in the bathroom. The arm allows you to position the mirror to help you see. They're also used in some old-fashioned stores to get things out of the window that customers want to see more closely.

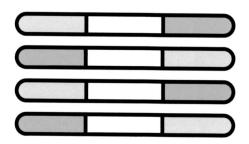

6 Repeat steps 1-5 using the other six sticks.

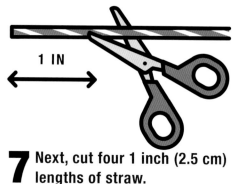

1 IN

7 Next, cut four 1 inch (2.5 cm) lengths of straw.

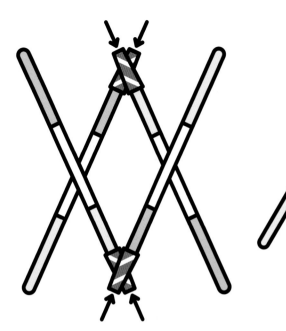

8 Arrange the sticks into two "Xs," then push the bits of straw onto the ends of the four sticks that cross in the middle.

9 Take the first set of sticks and use the second skewer to make a hole in the tape between the two sticks. Repeat for the other three sets of sticks.

Inside the engineering

This contraption works because the little bits of skewer act as hinges. A hinge is a type of joint that attaches two things together while allowing for limited movement. The hinges in your Engineer's Arm allow the craft sticks that form the arm to extend, so you can grab things that would normally be out of reach.

10 Then make a hole in the middle of each bit of straw.

11 Cut four short lengths of skewer and poke them through the holes you've just made in the sticks and straws. The skewers join the arms together.

12 To form the grabber, cut two short lengths from the final craft stick. Use the glue gun to stick them onto the ends of the arm at right angles.

13 Once the grabber is dry, squeeze together the two sticks at the other end to extend the arm and grab small objects!

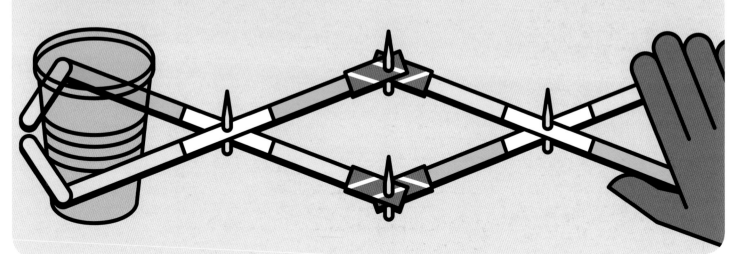

THE BOUNCING BRIDGE

How is it possible to hold up an entire bridge with just a few cables? Make this "bouncing" bridge and find out for yourself!

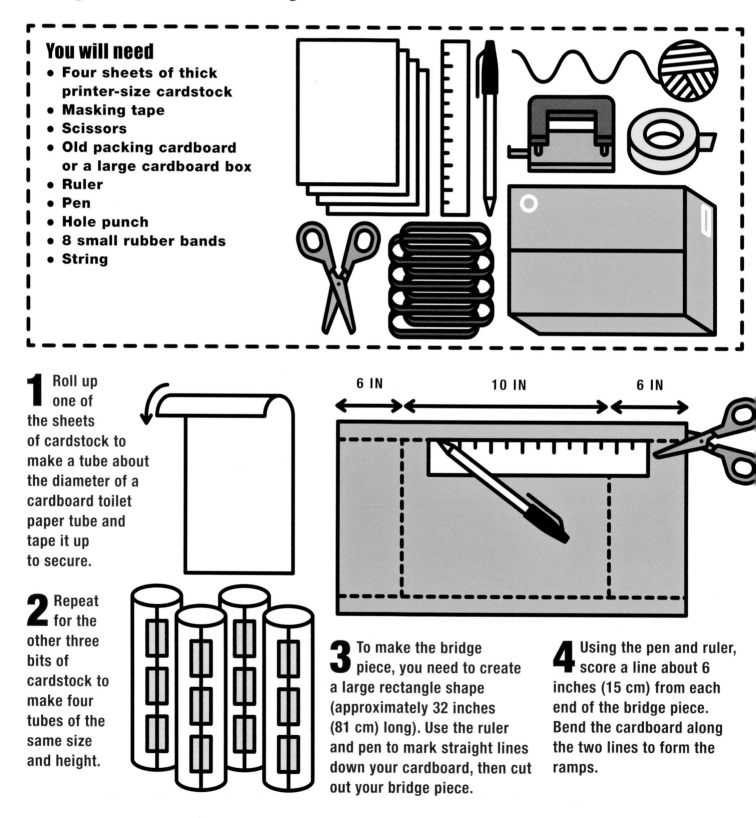

You will need
- **Four sheets of thick printer-size cardstock**
- **Masking tape**
- **Scissors**
- **Old packing cardboard or a large cardboard box**
- **Ruler**
- **Pen**
- **Hole punch**
- **8 small rubber bands**
- **String**

1 Roll up one of the sheets of cardstock to make a tube about the diameter of a cardboard toilet paper tube and tape it up to secure.

2 Repeat for the other three bits of cardstock to make four tubes of the same size and height.

6 IN | 10 IN | 6 IN

3 To make the bridge piece, you need to create a large rectangle shape (approximately 32 inches (81 cm) long). Use the ruler and pen to mark straight lines down your cardboard, then cut out your bridge piece.

4 Using the pen and ruler, score a line about 6 inches (15 cm) from each end of the bridge piece. Bend the cardboard along the two lines to form the ramps.

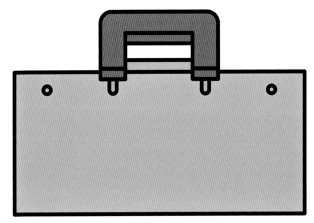

5 Next, cut two strips of cardstock to make a base for your towers. The strips should be about 8 inches (20 cm) longer than the width of the bridge's ramps and a little over 3 inches (about 8 cm) wide.

6 Tape a tube to the first strip of cardstock. Make it stand as upright as you can. Add a second tube to the other end of the cardstock, then repeat with the second strip of cardstock and the other tubes.

7 Use your hole punch to make holes along the edges of the bridge's base. Four or six holes on each edge is about right.

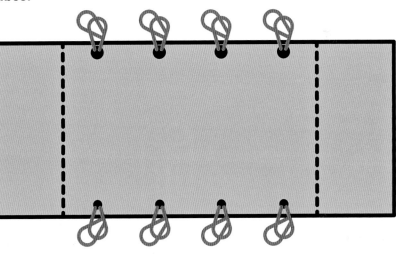

8 Thread the first rubber band through one of the holes you just made.

9 Thread the rubber band through itself and pull it tight to make a loop.

10 Repeat steps 8 and 9 and add rubber band loops to each of the other holes.

11 Cut two slits (approximately 1.5 inches (4 cm) long) in the first of your towers. The slits should line up with the corners of the base. Then repeat for the other three towers.

12 Cut a length of string 48 inches (122 cm) long and start to thread it through the rubber band loops. Take the end of the string and thread it up through the slits in your first tower and pull the string through.

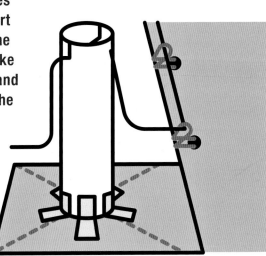

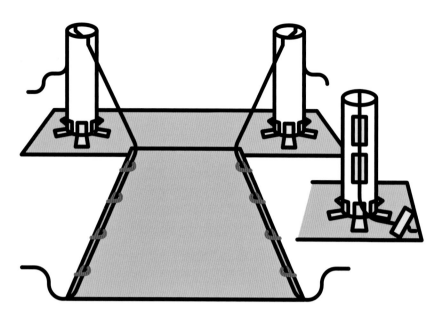

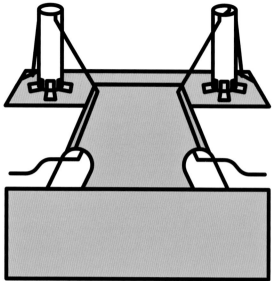

13 Do the same on the other side. You should now have two 48 inch (122 cm) lengths of string (one on each side of the bridge) threaded through the rubber bands and pulled up through the towers at one end.

14 Now tape the string to the base next to the two towers to secure.

15 At the other end of the bridge, pull the string through the slits in the other two towers and lay them down flat on the table.

16 Then go back to yor first towers and secure the base by taping it to the table.

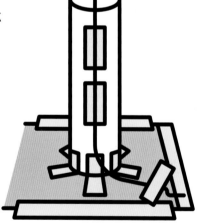

In the real world

There are suspension bridges all over the world. Some, like the Golden Gate Bridge in San Francisco, are really famous, but clever engineers have been making them for hundreds of years. In Peru, South America, there's a suspension bridge made out of twisted grass that's more than 500 years old!

17 Here's where you may need either an adult—or just another pair of hands. Raise the two towers at the other end of the bridge and tape them to the table as well.

18 To make your bridge "float" in the air, you may have to adjust the string by pulling it tighter through the slits and wrapping it around your towers to secure. Once you've got the balance right, tape down the loose string to the final two towers (as per step 14). Your bridge is held up only by two bits of string!

19 Tape down the ends of the bridge to make a secure ramp for any vehicles to travel over it!

Inside the engineering

You've built a suspension bridge! Suspension bridges are clever because they can be built across a river or canyon without using towers all the way across to support. Instead, engineers string cables along the bridge and then up and through the tops of the towers at either end. This lets the towers take the weight of the bridge—and that weight pushes down on the towers and into the ground. The bottom of each tower is usually buried deep into the ground for extra strength and the ends of each cable are anchored securely. The other neat thing about suspension bridges is that they're not rigid, so they can sometimes even stay standing during an earthquake.

WOW!

WEATHER VANE

Which way is the wind blowing? Make this simple weather vane to find out!

You will need
- Piece of printer-size cardstock
- Plastic straw
- Scissors
- Plastic bowl or paper plate
- Paper cup
- Hot glue gun
- Ruler
- Pencil with eraser on the end
- Pin
- Magnetic compass
- Craft knife

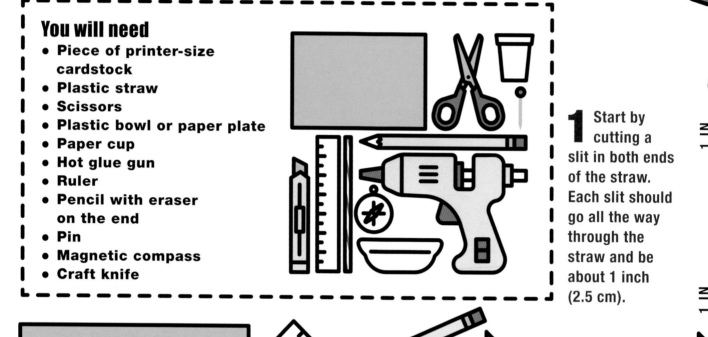

1 Start by cutting a slit in both ends of the straw. Each slit should go all the way through the straw and be about 1 inch (2.5 cm).

1 IN
1 IN

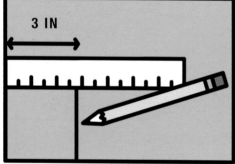

3 IN

2 Use your ruler to mark out a square on the card, with sides that are 3 inches (8 cm) long. Cut it out.

3 With the ruler, draw a line from one corner of the square to the opposite corner. Cut along the line to make two identical triangles.

4 Slot one triangle into each end of the straw. The triangles should be pointing in the same direction.

In the real world

You'll find weather vanes—sometimes called wind vanes or weathercocks—all over the place. They're especially important for farmers who need to know how the wind and the weather is going to affect the crops they're trying to grow.

5 Ask an adult to make a hole in the bottom of the cup with a craft knife. They should make it small to start with, then carefully adjust the size so the pencil fits inside it securely and stands upright.

N
W   E
S

6 Turn the bowl (or plate) upside down and write N, E, S, and W to mark the four points of the compass.

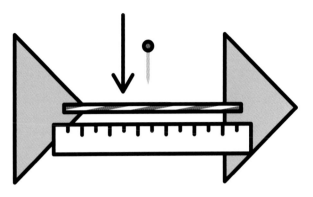

7 Apply some glue to the rim of the cup and stick it to the center of the bowl.

8 Slot the pencil into the hole.

9 Measure halfway along the straw and poke the pin through it. Mind your fingers!

10 Push the pin down into the eraser on the pencil and give it a spin. You'll need a compass to make sure your N, S, E, and W marks are lined up correctly but after that your weather vane will spin and tell you which way the wind is blowing. Cool!

Inside the engineering

This project is another example of a simple machine, in this case a wheel and axle. The straw is the wheel and the pin is the axle that it spins around.

MAGNETIC SPINNER

Here's how to make an intriguing spinning toy with a few empty cans, a magnet, and a few old nuts.

You will need
- 6 empty aluminum drink cans, all the same size
- Craft knife
- Scissors
- Strong magnet
- A few metal nuts
- Hot glue gun
- Felt pen

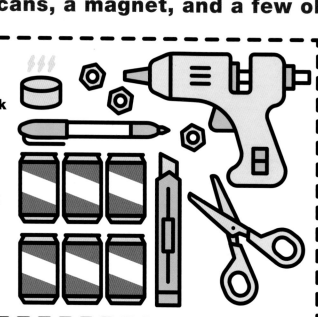

1 Get an adult to cut into the first can with a knife, then use the scissors to cut the bottom of the can off.

Do not try to do this yourself— cut cans are razor-sharp.

2 Now your adult needs to cut around the very bottom of the can and trim any sharp edges until you're left with a flat, round disc.

3 Repeat steps 1–2 with the other five cans until you have six identical discs.

4 Take your magnet and glue it into the bottom of the first disc.

5 Put glue around the edge of one of the other discs, then push them together to make a flying saucer shape.

6 Take a felt pen and mark around the edge of your flying saucer. This allows you to tell which one has the magnet inside.

7 Glue a nut into one of the other discs. If the nuts are small enough, glue more than one.

8 Glue another disc on top to make a flying saucer shape, then use the last two discs to make another flying saucer with nuts inside. You now have two with nuts inside and one with a magnet.

Troubleshooting

If your flying saucers aren't spinning as fast or for as long as you'd like, try them on a different surface, such as a glass table or a shiny kitchen worktop. If you want to balance three on top of one another, make a little dent in one side of each of the two flying saucers with nuts inside them. Balance them on top of the magnet saucer with the dent facing down.

9 Put one of the nut flying saucers on top of the magnet flying saucer, then try spinning the one with the magnet and watch what happens.

10 Carefully add the other nut flying saucer and see if you can get all three spinning at once!

COOL!

Inside the engineering

The strong magnet inside one of the flying saucers is powerful enough to exert a magnetic force on the nuts inside the others. The spinning motion helps to stabilize the flying saucers to create this unusual and intricate balancing act.

DOUBLE CUP FLYER

**Want to make the world's weirdest-looking plane?
You won't believe how well this odd contraption flies!**

You will need
- **Two identical plastic cups**
- **Strong tape**
- **Four long rubber bands**

1 Tear off a strip of tape and attach it to the bottom of one of the cups. It should go about halfway around the cup.

2 Place the cup upside down on a flat surface and put the bottom of the other cup on top, so that the two bottom ends line up perfectly. Press the tape into place, making sure you have a good join.

3 Continue wrapping layers of tape around the join until it feels good and solid—this "plane" is going to get bashed around a lot!

4 Take two of the rubber bands and join them together. You need to loop the first band through the second band, then loop it through itself.

5 Join the other two rubber bands to the first two in the same way. You should now have a long "chain."

6 Use your thumb to hold one end of the chain in place, right on the join of the flyer.

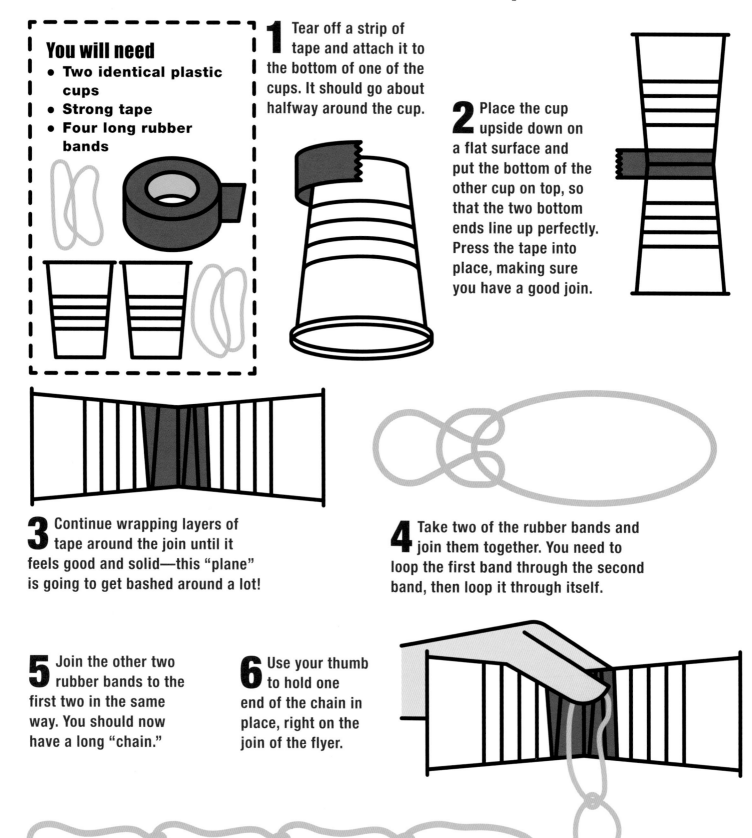

Inside the engineering

This plane can fly thanks to something called the Magnus effect. As the cups travel through the air, their backspin causes air pressure to be lower on the top side of the cups. The higher pressure underneath the cups gives a lifting force to keep the cups aloft. The same effect causes a spinning soccer ball or table tennis ball to swerve in the air.

7 Take the other end of the rubber band and wrap it under the cups and away from you, then back over the cups toward you. Keep wrapping until there is just a short length left, which you can hold in your other hand.

8 Keep holding the rubber band firmly around the cup with one hand. Use your other hand to pull the other end of the rubber band out in front of you, as if you were priming a catapult.

Take it further
Try launching your flyer from an upstairs window or other high place and see how much farther it can fly.

9 Let go of the cup and as you do, sweep your other hand down to get it out of the way. The cups will spin like crazy and fly for a remarkably long distance!

WOW!

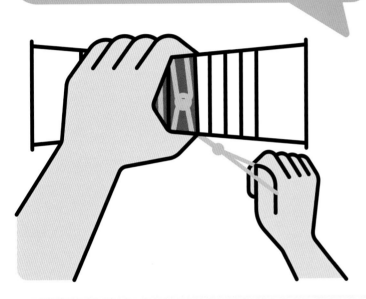

MARBLE ROLLER COASTER

What goes up must come down. It can also go around and around, over bridges, and through tunnels!

You will need

- **Three lengths of polyethylene pipe insulation**
- **Cardboard mailing tube (a bit wider than the insulating tubes)**
- **Plastic cup**
- **Scissors**
- **Masking tape**
- **Small marble**
- **Books, DVDs, or other household objects for supporting a track**

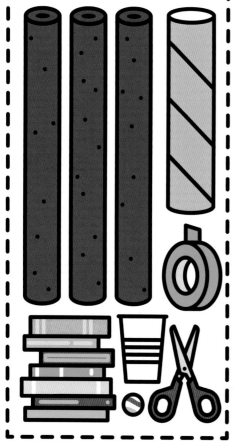

1 The pipe insulation should have a slit in one side. Use your thumb to open the slit in the first tube, from one end to the other.

2 Using the open slit as a guide, cut through the other side of the tube. You should end up with two long halfpipe shapes.

3 Repeat steps 1 and 2 with the other two pipes, so that you have six identical halfpipes. These are your tracks.

4 Make a pile of books or DVDs on a table. Rest the first piece of track on it.

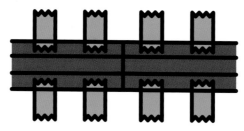

5 Tape the bottom of the track to the table and join the next piece of track to it. Make sure that none of the tape will get in the way of a rolling marble.

Take it further

Experiment with your roller coaster by adjusting the height of the first slope. You could also remove the bridge or change other parts of the track.

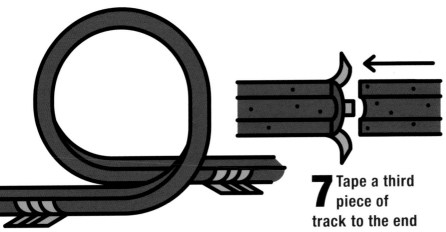

6 Take the second bit of track and loop it over. Ask a friend to hold it in position while you tape it down.

7 Tape a third piece of track to the end of the loop and then use tape to connect a fourth piece to the other end.

Inside the engineering

Lifting the ball to the top of the track gives it an energy store. This store makes the ball roll faster as it goes down the slope. If it enters the loop fast enough, its energy store is big enough to make it loop the loop. The marble eventually stops rolling because it transfers its energy store to the air and track.

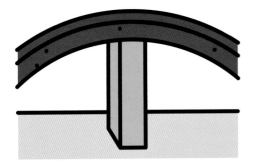

8 Put something underneath this long section of track to create a "bridge" section. The track now goes down, does a loop-the-loop, then goes up and over a bridge.

9 Attach the last two sections of tubing to the end. Slide the cardboard mailing tube over this section of track to make a tunnel.

10 Bend your track up at the end to rest on a short stack of books or DVDs. Put a cup at the end to catch the marble.

11 Try running a marble down your finished track. You can lift the first section of track up if needed to give the marble enough oomph to make it around the loop and over the bridge.

CLOTHESLINE FLYER

Here's how to make a plane that flies along a clothesline. String it up in your back yard and watch it go!

You will need
- 8 craft sticks
- Hot glue gun
- Large rubber band
- Four paper clips
- Masking tape
- Ruler
- Small nail
- Old ballpoint pen
- Plastic soda bottle
- Craft knife
- Awl, or something to make a hole with
- Drawing pins
- Sheet of printer-size cardstock
- String

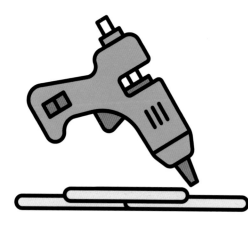

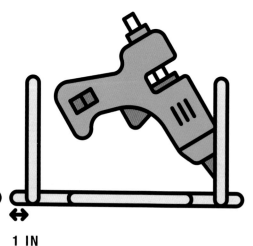

1 IN

1 Start by making a frame for your flyer. Lay two craft sticks end to end, then glue a third stick on top of them.

2 Glue two more sticks at right angles. They should be about 1 inch (2.5 cm) in from either end.

3 Glue another stick at an angle in one corner to brace your flyer and give it strength. Then do the same at the other corner.

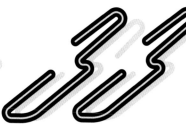

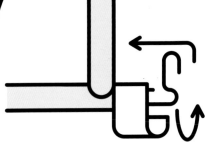

4 Carefully bend one of the paper clips open, then set it aside.

5 Take the other two paper clips, bend them open completely, and then twist one half of each paper clip 90 degrees.

6 Glue the paper clip from step 4 to the back end of the flyer.

7 Wrap it securely with tape and then bend it back in toward the frame.

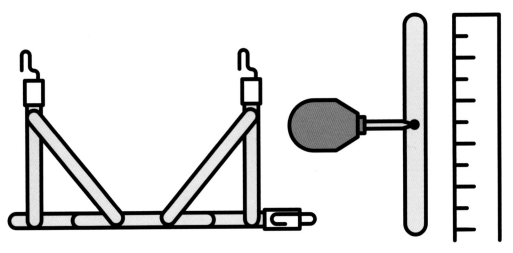

8 Glue and tape the other two paper clips to the top sticks. They should be lined up in the same direction, so they can hook over the clothesline together.

9 Now it's time to make the propeller. Use your ruler to find the middle of the final craft stick and then make a small hole in the center.

10 Cut the top section out of a large plastic bottle, then cut that in half and then cut out two curved strips. These will be your propeller blades.

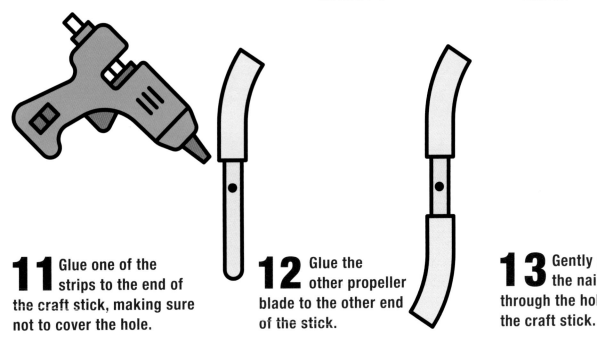
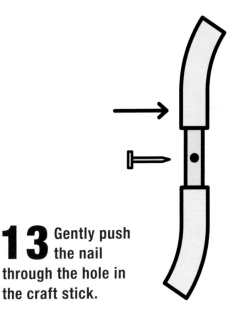

11 Glue one of the strips to the end of the craft stick, making sure not to cover the hole.

12 Glue the other propeller blade to the other end of the stick.

13 Gently push the nail through the hole in the craft stick.

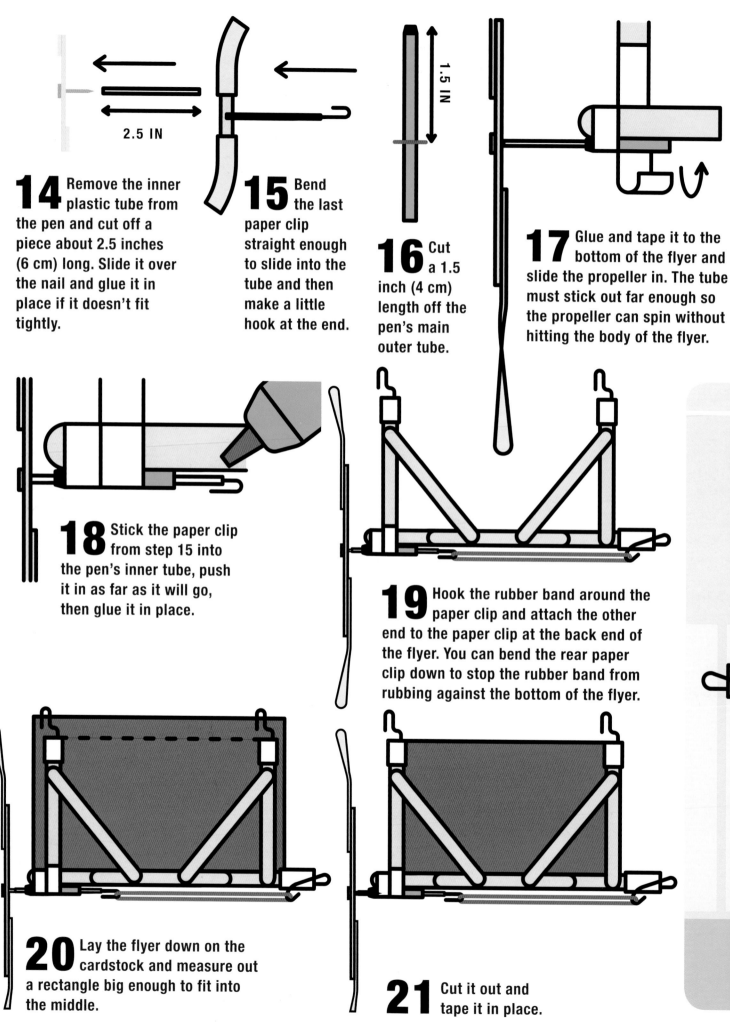

14 Remove the inner plastic tube from the pen and cut off a piece about 2.5 inches (6 cm) long. Slide it over the nail and glue it in place if it doesn't fit tightly.

2.5 IN

15 Bend the last paper clip straight enough to slide into the tube and then make a little hook at the end.

1.5 IN

16 Cut a 1.5 inch (4 cm) length off the pen's main outer tube.

17 Glue and tape it to the bottom of the flyer and slide the propeller in. The tube must stick out far enough so the propeller can spin without hitting the body of the flyer.

18 Stick the paper clip from step 15 into the pen's inner tube, push it in as far as it will go, then glue it in place.

19 Hook the rubber band around the paper clip and attach the other end to the paper clip at the back end of the flyer. You can bend the rear paper clip down to stop the rubber band from rubbing against the bottom of the flyer.

20 Lay the flyer down on the cardstock and measure out a rectangle big enough to fit into the middle.

21 Cut it out and tape it in place.

22 Cut a long piece of string and tie each end to something stable, so that you have a level line. Use the two paper clips at the top of the flyer to hook it over the string.

23 Twist the propeller to wind the flyer up. The more you wind it, the farther and faster it will shoot along the string. When you're ready, let go of the propeller and watch it go!

Take it further

Want to make your flyer move even faster?
• Swap the string for fishing line to reduce friction.
• Use two rubber bands instead of one.
• Experiment with a different propeller shape and see if that boosts your speed.

Inside the engineering

As you wind up the rubber band by turning the propeller, the elastic becomes an energy store. When you release the propeller this energy store makes the propeller turn. The turning propeller acts like a screw, creating thrust that pushes the flyer forward.

ELECTRIC SPINNER

Can you make a simple motor that spins really fast with just a battery, a magnet, and a piece of wire? Of course you can!

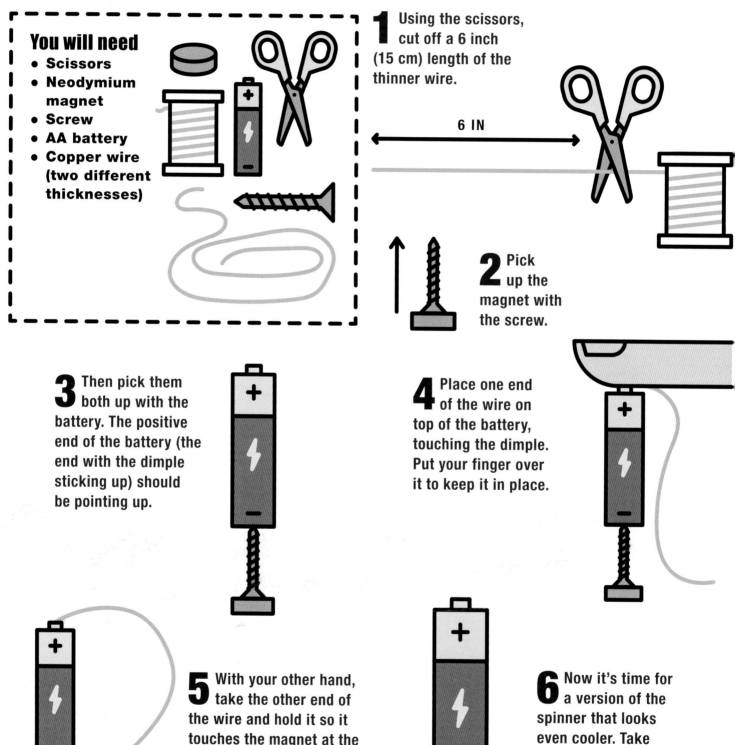

You will need
- Scissors
- Neodymium magnet
- Screw
- AA battery
- Copper wire (two different thicknesses)

1 Using the scissors, cut off a 6 inch (15 cm) length of the thinner wire.

6 IN

2 Pick up the magnet with the screw.

3 Then pick them both up with the battery. The positive end of the battery (the end with the dimple sticking up) should be pointing up.

4 Place one end of the wire on top of the battery, touching the dimple. Put your finger over it to keep it in place.

5 With your other hand, take the other end of the wire and hold it so it touches the magnet at the bottom. You may have to experiment a little to get the position right. When you do, the magnet will begin to spin quickly.

6 Now it's time for a version of the spinner that looks even cooler. Take everything apart and stick the battery directly on top of the magnet, leaving the screw out.

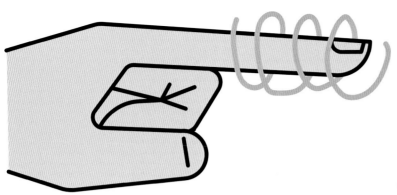

7 Cut an an 8 inch (20 cm) length of the thicker wire and start to wrap it around your finger. Since this loop must be wide enough to spin around the magnet, you may need to use your adult assistant's finger!

8 Keep wrapping until you end up with a kind of spiral or cone shape that's a bit wider at the bottom. Bend the very end of the top over so it points downward.

9 Drop the wire over the battery and let go. You may need to adjust the shape of the spinner to get the connections just right but when you do, it will spin REALLY fast.

Troubleshooting

If your spinner doesn't spin, it may be that your wire is coated. Ask an adult to burn the ends with a lighter and scrape off the coating. Then try it again.

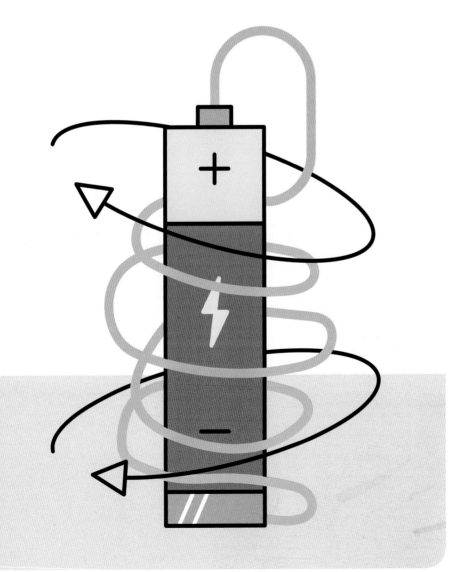

Inside the engineering

By touching the top of the battery with one end of the wire and the magnet with the other, you're creating a circuit that lets electricity run through the wire. When that electricity moves through the field created by the magnet it creates a force which causes the magnet to spin. In the second version of the device, the wire spins. This device is called a homopolar motor.

PAPER POPPER

Do you want to turn a sheet of paper into something that makes an almighty racket? Silly question! Who wouldn't want to try that?

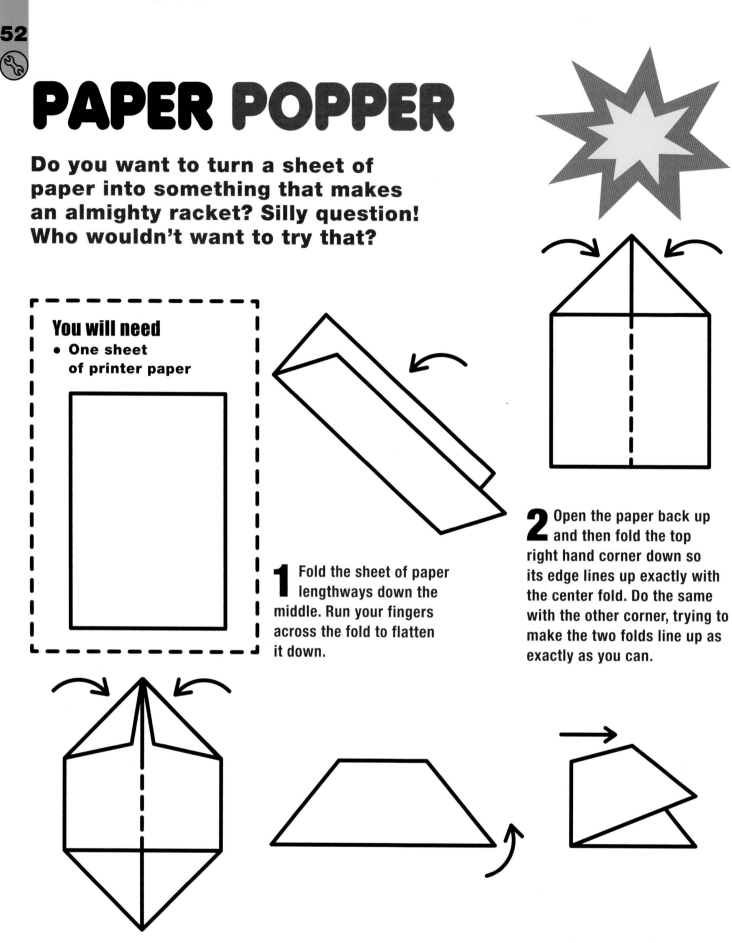

You will need
- One sheet of printer paper

1 Fold the sheet of paper lengthways down the middle. Run your fingers across the fold to flatten it down.

2 Open the paper back up and then fold the top right hand corner down so its edge lines up exactly with the center fold. Do the same with the other corner, trying to make the two folds line up as exactly as you can.

3 Turn the paper around and make exactly the same folds at the other end—you'll end up with a sort of diamond shape. Flatten all the folds carefully.

4 Rotate the paper one quarter-turn and then fold it in half, using the fold you made in step 1.

5 Fold one side of the shape from left to right so that it lines up with the other side. Flatten the fold.

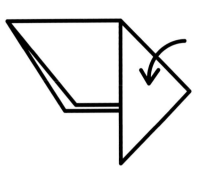

6 Open the shape back up and turn it 180 degrees, so the short side is on the bottom and the long side is at the top.

7 Take the point at the top right and fold it down so the top edge lines up with the center fold. The point will stick out below the bottom of the shape.

Take it further You can use your popper again if you take the fold of paper that's popped out and push it back into the center. For a louder noise, try using a sheet of newspaper. It won't last as long but because the fold is bigger and the paper is thinner, more air will be forced in and it'll make a bang, rather than a pop.

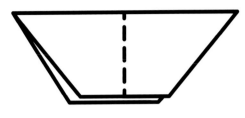

Inside the engineering

The popper works because of air pressure. When you swipe the popper down, air is forced into the fold of paper in the middle, forcing it to open so quickly that it makes a distinctive popping sound.

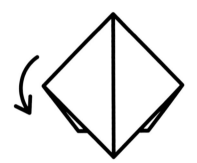

8 Do the same with the other corner. Try to make sure the two points line up at the bottom and that each fold is nice and flat.

9 Flip the popper over and fold it in half down the vertical line. Grasp the two points at the bottom, making sure you're not holding the paper folds in the middle.

10 To use the popper, raise it above your head and bring it down as fast as you can—as if you were throwing a dart at the ground in front of you. It will make a loud popping sound as the folded paper in the center is forced open.

POP!

ROBOT ARTIST

Do you think a robot can make art? Now's your chance to find out!

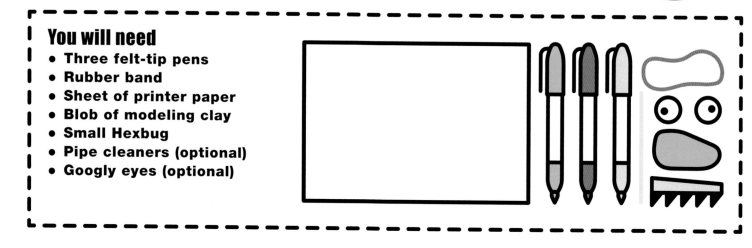

You will need
- **Three felt-tip pens**
- **Rubber band**
- **Sheet of printer paper**
- **Blob of modeling clay**
- **Small Hexbug**
- **Pipe cleaners (optional)**
- **Googly eyes (optional)**

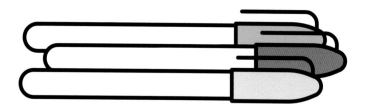

1 Hold the three pens together so their bottom ends form a triangle.

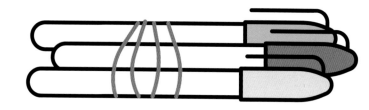

2 Put the rubber band around them and loop it over and over until they're held tightly together.

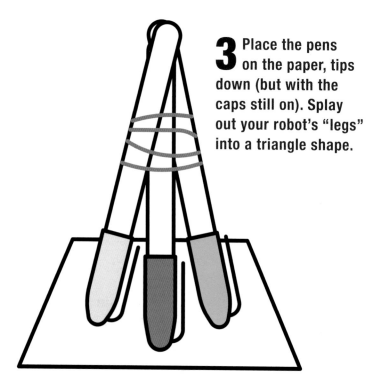

3 Place the pens on the paper, tips down (but with the caps still on). Splay out your robot's "legs" into a triangle shape.

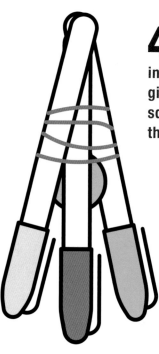

4 Jam some of the modeling clay up in between them and give everything a good squeeze. This will keep the "legs" apart.

5 Use another blob of clay to attach the Hexbug to the side of the robot, just below the rubber band. The Hexbug's legs should be pointing outward, so you can see the little switch on the bottom.

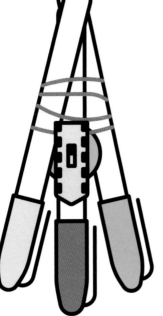

6 Take the tops off the pens and put your robot back onto the sheet of paper.

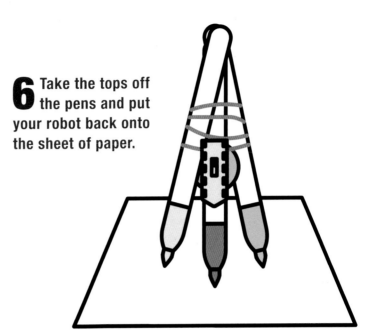

7 Turn the bug on to start its motor. If the surface is completely flat, it will begin to draw circles.

Take it further You can make your robot artist look cooler by decorating it. Wrap a pipe cleaner around the top end (above the rubber band) and stick in smaller pieces of pipe cleaner to make some hair. Finish it off with the googly eyes!

Inside the engineering

The electric motor inside the Hexbug makes it vibrate really quickly. Because it's attached to the pens, these vibrations pass through the modeling clay and on to the pens. Your robot keeps trying to draw circles because of its triangular shape. It is much easier for a robot of this shape to turn in a circle than it is to follow a straight line.

THE BOTTLE ROCKET

A quick raid on the kitchen cupboard will help you build a bottle rocket that shoots high into the air!

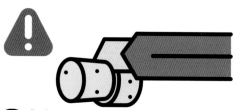

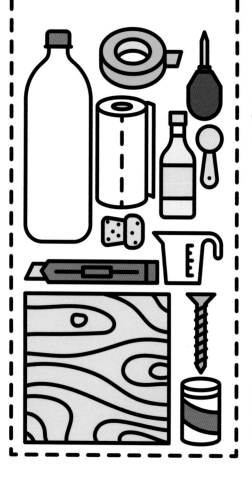

1 Get an adult to screw the screw into the center of the wood. The end of the screw should stick out the other side.

2 Ask an adult to cut the round part off the top of the cork. Test the bottom half to check that the narrower end fits snugly into the end of the plastic bottle. If it's loose, wrap tape around the cork until you get a snug fit.

3 Screw the cork onto the end of the screw, until the wider end of the cork touches the wood.

4 Fill the measuring cup with water until you have a little over 1 1/2 cups, then pour it into the bottle.

5 Measure out 3/4 cup of vinegar and pour that into the bottle as well.

6 Lay out your paper towel. Spoon out two tablespoons of baking soda in a line along the top edge.

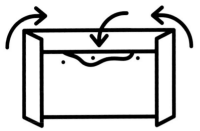

7 Fold the top of the towel over the baking soda, then fold the left and right sides in.

8 Roll the towel up, from top to bottom. It must be tight enough to fit easily inside the bottle.

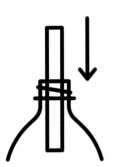

9 Take the bottle, the towel of baking soda, and the wooden square outside. Get your assistant to drop the towel into the bottle.

10 Have your assistant place the board over the top of the bottle so that the cork gets wedged into the bottle's neck.

11 Quickly flip the whole thing over so that the bottle is upside down, pointing straight up. Get your assistant to push down on the bottle again to make sure the cork is in nice and tight.

12 Stand back! After a few seconds, the bottle will explode off the cork and fly straight up in the air, just like a real rocket.

Inside the engineering

The baking soda and vinegar react to produce carbon dioxide gas. The pressure inside the bottle increases until it pushes the cork out. The pressure forces the water and vinegar out, putting an upward force on the bottle. This makes it accelerate upward, which is an example of Newton's third law—for every action there is an equal and opposite reaction.

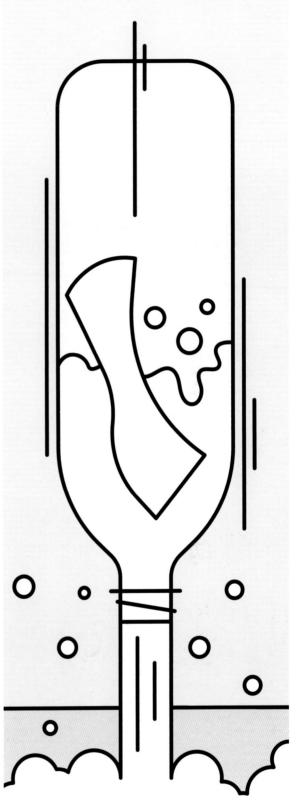

THE MARBLE MAZE

Marble maze games can drive you crazy. And now, thanks to this simple project, you can make your own!

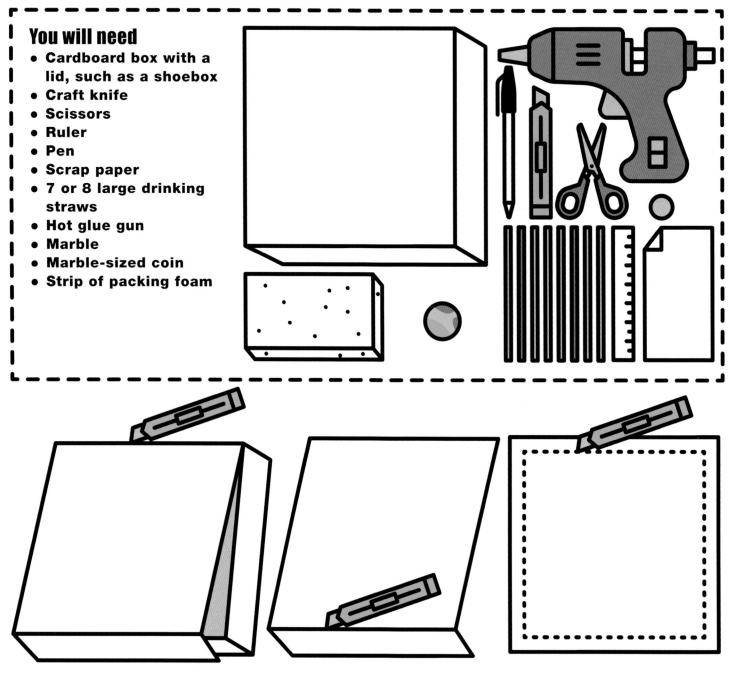

You will need
- **Cardboard box with a lid, such as a shoebox**
- **Craft knife**
- **Scissors**
- **Ruler**
- **Pen**
- **Scrap paper**
- **7 or 8 large drinking straws**
- **Hot glue gun**
- **Marble**
- **Marble-sized coin**
- **Strip of packing foam**

1 If your box's lid is attached, ask an adult to cut it off with a craft knife. If you can't find a box with its own lid, find a piece of cardboard that is slightly bigger than the box.

2 Cut round any edges on the lid until you have a flat piece of cardboard that will sit on top of the box.

3 Ask an adult to carefully trim the lid's edge with the craft knife so that it fits snugly inside the box. Cut off little strips at a time, testing the fit after each one.

4 Use the ruler and pen to draw a square in one corner of the box. It should be big enough for the marble to go through it. This is the hole where the marble will come out when it falls through the maze.

5 Ask an adult to cut out the square with the craft knife.

6 Measure out four equal pieces of packing foam to make the supports, then cut them apart. They must all be the same height and small enough to fit in the box.

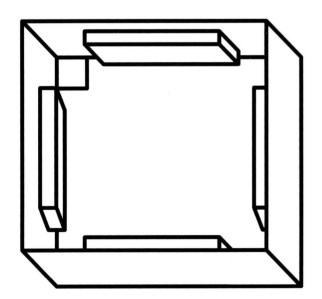

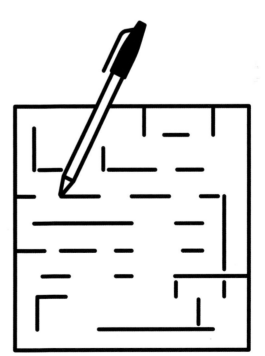

7 Apply glue to the bottom and side of the first piece, then stick it into the box. It should be in the middle of one of the four sides. Repeat step 7 for the other three support pieces.

8 Sketch out a maze design on the scrap paper. Don't make it too complicated, or the maze will be too difficult. Test your design to make sure there is a route to the exit!

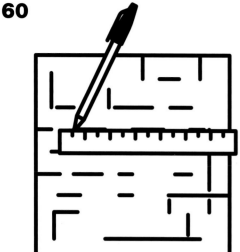

9 When you're happy with your design, copy it onto the cardboard lid, using the ruler to keep the lines straight. They will be your "walls," so make sure there is enough space between them for the marble to fit easily. You can use a marble-sized coin to measure the space.

10 To make it more fun, add a few traps for the marble—but not on the exit route! Draw around the coin, then ask an adult to cut the holes out.

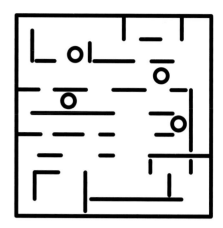

11 The finished maze plan, complete with walls, holes, and marble, should look like this.

Inside the engineering

This project makes use of the ramp, one of the six simple machines. Ramps (sometimes called "inclined planes") make it easier to move heavy objects from one height to another. When you hold the maze flat, the marble will not move. When you tip (or incline) the maze in a particular direction, the marble will move in that direction because it's moving downhill. By moving the box around to make the marble move in different directions, you're just changing the orientation of the inclined plane.

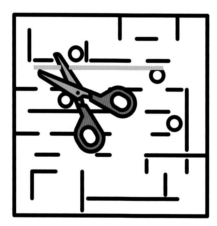

12 Measure a straw against the first line and then cut it to size with the scissors.

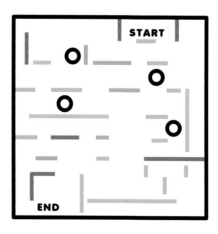

14 Label the "START" and "END" of your maze route.

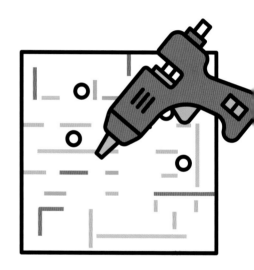

13 Cut the rest of the straw pieces, then glue them into place.

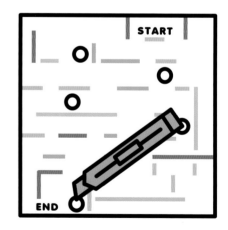

15 Add another hole at the end so that the marble can fall through and come out of the hole you made in the base in step 5.

16 Carefully take your maze and put it inside the box. Push down until you feel it come to rest on top of the supports you made in steps 6 and 7.

17 Pop the marble into the maze at the start. Tilt the box from side to side to make the marble move, and see how long it takes you to get to the end. Watch out for the traps!

Take it further It's easy to make the maze more difficult. Just ease it out of the box and get your assistant to make some more holes!

18 When you get to the end, roll the marble into the hole and it will pop right out of the bottom of the box!

SUPERSONIC STRAW

Here's how to transform a simple drinking straw into a powerful rocket that flies fast and straight.

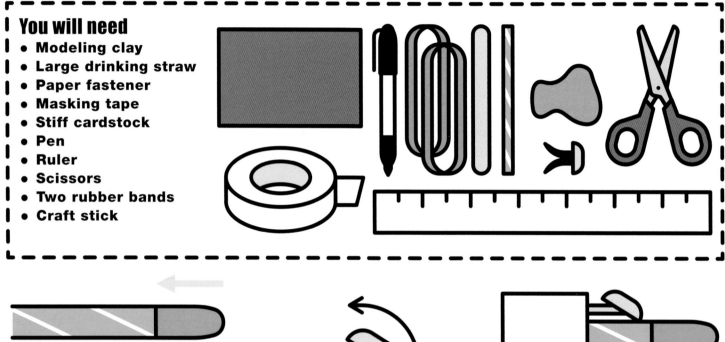

You will need
- Modeling clay
- Large drinking straw
- Paper fastener
- Masking tape
- Stiff cardstock
- Pen
- Ruler
- Scissors
- Two rubber bands
- Craft stick

1 Roll a small piece of modeling clay until it's about 1 inch (2.5 cm) long and thin enough to fit inside the straw. Leave a bit sticking out and mold this into the rocket's nose cone.

2 Bend the paper fastener's head so it sits at an angle.

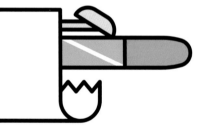

3 Place the fastener against the straw, then use the tape to attach it. Add another piece of tape to secure.

4 Next, cut out two pieces of cardstock—each 1 by 1.5 inches (2.5 by 4 cm). Draw a line diagonally across each and cut along the line to make triangle shapes.

1 IN

1.5 IN

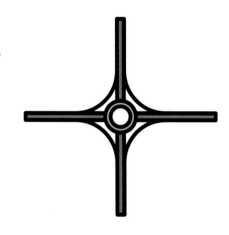

5 Tape one triangle to the back end of the straw to make the first fin. Tape the cardstock on both sides to help keep it straight.

6 Attach the three other triangles in the same way to form an "X" shape.

In the real world

Rocket shapes haven't changed very much since the first modern ones flew about 80 years ago. That's because the shape of the rocket and the arrangement of fins are very efficient at allowing it to fly through the air in a straight line.

7 Next, take your two rubber bands and loop them together.

8 Then pull them tight to form one long rubber band.

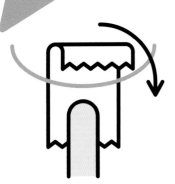

9 Take the craft stick, tear off a bit of tape, and place the end of the craft stick on top of the tape. Then lay the rubber band on the tape.

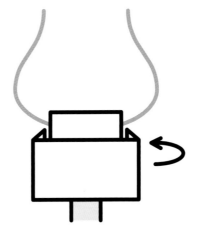

10 Fold the tape over to secure the rubber band. Add a second bit of tape to help keep the rubber band in place.

Inside the engineering

Adding modeling clay to the tip of the rocket gives it weight. Forming it into a "nose" makes the straw more aerodynamic so it flies through the air faster. The fins stop it from wobbling off course, so it goes farther. The rubber band stores potential energy when you pull it back and transfers it to the rocket as kinetic energy when you let go.

11 Hold the craft stick in one hand and loop the rubber band over the paper fastener on the straw. Pull back gently, then release the straw "rocket" and watch it fly! As you release the straw, remember to lower the hand holding your craft stick so the rocket doesn't hit it.

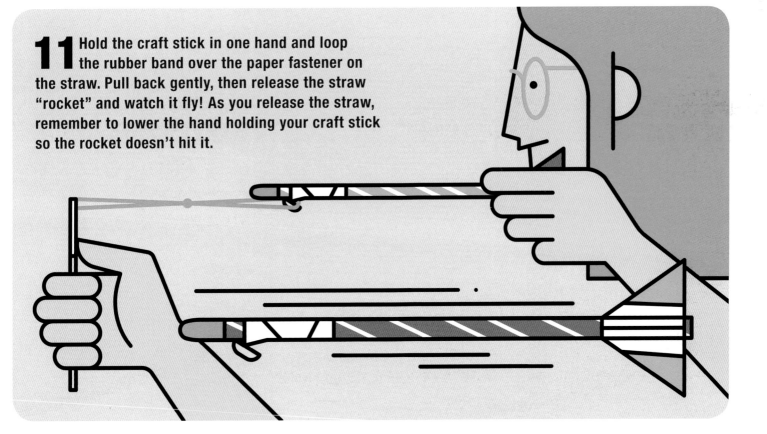

THE DANCING ROBOT

Amaze your friends by making a robot spin around the table without you even touching it. It's all thanks to the power of magnetism!

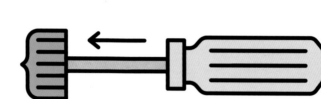

1 The bottle cap will spin better if it has a small dimple poking out the bottom. Some already have one, but if yours doesn't, make one with the screwdriver.

2 Glue one of the magnets to the inside of the bottle cap.

3 Press the modeling clay into the middle of the magnet.

4 Fold the printer paper into quarters and then cut them out, so you have four identical rectangles. You only need two, so put two of the rectangles aside.

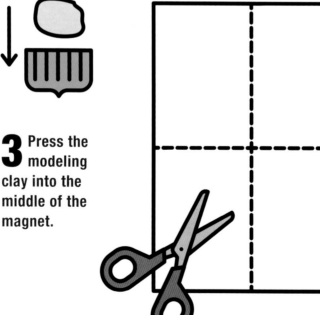

5 Draw a robot on one of the paper rectangles, or use sticky-backed shapes instead. Then make another robot on one of the other pieces of paper.

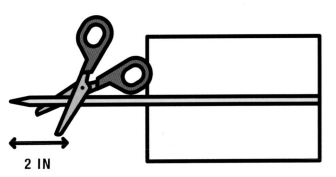

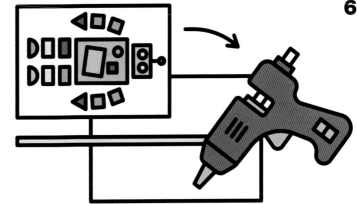

6 Lay the skewer on the back of one of your robots, with the blunt end level with the top of the paper. Cut the pointed end off, about 2 inches (5 cm) from the point.

2 IN

7 Glue the skewer in place, then add glue around the edges of the paper and stick the other piece on. There should be a robot showing on each side.

8 Push the stick into the modeling clay and stand your robot up.

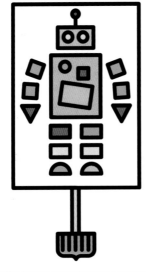

9 Place two magnets at one end of the ruler—one above it and one below.

10 Push the ruler gently toward the robot and it should start to spin. If it is attracted to the ruler instead, just flip the ruler over and try again.

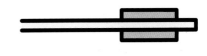

Take it further You can make many different spinners by changing the top part, while leaving the cap, magnet, and modeling clay as they are.

Inside the engineering

A magnet has two ends, called poles—one north and one south. A north pole will attract another magnet's south pole, but it will repel (push away) another north pole. Pushing the magnets on the ruler toward the magnet on the robot transfers energy to it. This energy would usually repel the robot, but the dimple makes it easier to spin around than to slide away. You need to keep transferring energy to the robot by pushing the ruler toward the spinning robot. After that, inertia helps to keep it spinning.

THE BOTTLE SUB

In this project we'll show you how to make an underwater vehicle that rises and falls in water, just like a real submarine.

You will need

- Empty 2 liter plastic bottle
- Waterproof tape
- Something heavy—such as an old wrench
- Craft knife
- Awl, or something to make a hole with
- Scissors
- Plastic tubing

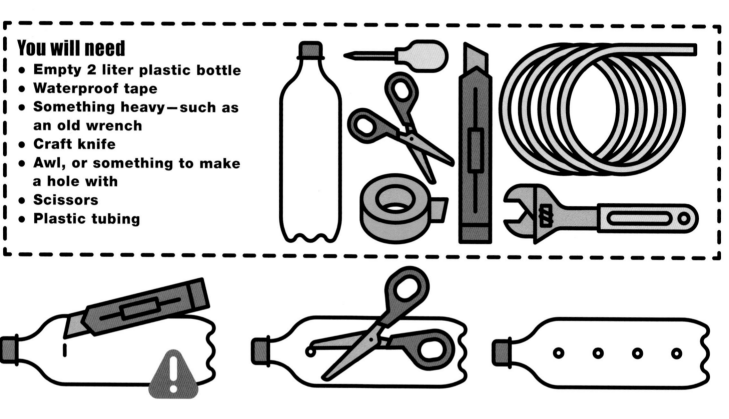

1 Start by getting an adult to make a little nick in the empty bottle with the craft knife.

2 Use the scissors to cut a small hole, about the size of a small coin.

3 Make three more holes in exactly the same way so that they run in a line along the length of the bottle.

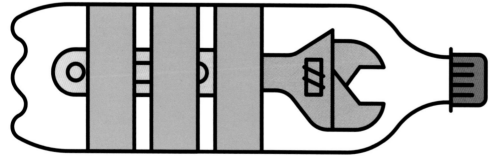

4 Take your heavy object and start to tape it to the bottle so it sits over the four holes you just made.

5 Next, take the cap from the bottle and poke a hole through it. Make sure that the hole matches the size of the plastic tubing you're going to use in the next step. Too small and it won't fit, too big and you'll have to seal it with glue.

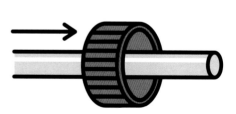

6 Poke one end of the tubing through the hole in the bottle cap—about 1 inch (2.5 cm) will do.

7 Screw the top back onto the bottle and pop it into the bathtub. You'll need to roll the bottle around a bit until the water pushes all the air out and it sinks.

8 Blow into the other end of the tube and you'll see the bottle rise through the water until it floats on the surface.

9 To make it sink again, suck the air out of the tube. Do this carefully or you'll end up with a mouthful of bath water! As you do, the "sub" will sink again.

Take it further Want to make the bottle look a bit more like a real sub? Use the scissors to cut a gentle curve out of an empty margarine or cream cheese tub. Glue it to the top of the bottle, then cut two short lengths of straw, bend one over to make a periscope, then glue them to the tub.

Inside the engineering

It's all about buoyancy. When there's no air inside the bottle, it sinks to the bottom of the bath, but when you blow into the bottle, the air pushes the water out and makes the "sub" float. Sucking air out of the tube lets the water come back in, so the "sub" sinks again.

THE HANGING ARCH

Ancient engineers built arches across roads—with no mortar to stick them together. Would you like to learn their secret?

You will need
- 6 sheets of printer-size cardstock
- Ruler
- Protractor, 4 inch (10 cm) size
- Pencil
- Scissors
- Clear tape

1 Draw a square in the center of a sheet of card, measuring 2 inches (5 cm) on each side. Make a little mark halfway along each side.

2 Place the protractor so that its baseline lines up with one of the square's sides and the "+" is over one of the marks. Make two marks, one at 75 degrees and one at 105 degrees.

3 Draw a line to join the two new marks together, then draw lines to join them to the top of the main square.

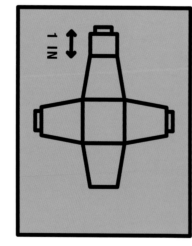

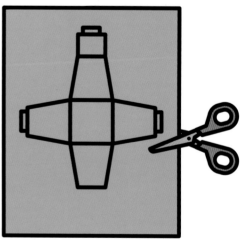

4 Repeat steps 2 and 3 on the other three sides of the square.

5 Draw a 1 inch (2.5 cm) square at the top of your shape, and add three small tabs to the top, left, and right sides.

6 Cut out your shape and use it as a template to draw five more. Draw lines between the different sections so you know where to fold the cardstock—then cut out the shapes.

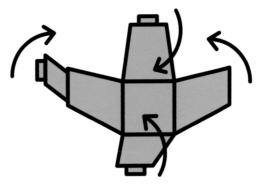

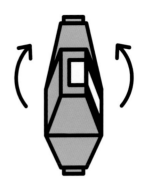

7 Use your scissors to score each shape along the lines where the different parts connect.

8 Fold the first block along the scored lines so the different sections (including the little tabs) fold inward.

9 Fold the top end over the opposite side and secure them with clear tape.

10 Connect the other two sides with tape to complete your first building block. Assemble the other five in the same way.

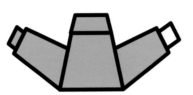

Inside the engineering

The arch stands up because of the way the final block—called the keystone—pushes on all the other blocks in the arch. The keystone not only fixes the structure in place, but by pushing outward through the arch and down into the ground, it also distributes the weight of the blocks more evenly.

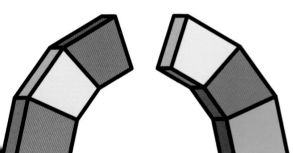

11 Place one of your building blocks on top of another. Ask a friend to hold three more blocks on the other side.

12 Carefully place the last block into position to complete the arch. You may need to brace each end with something heavy, but apart from that it will stand up completely on its own.

RUBBER BAND BOAT

Here's how to make a surprisingly powerful little boat with a "motor" made from craft sticks and a rubber band.

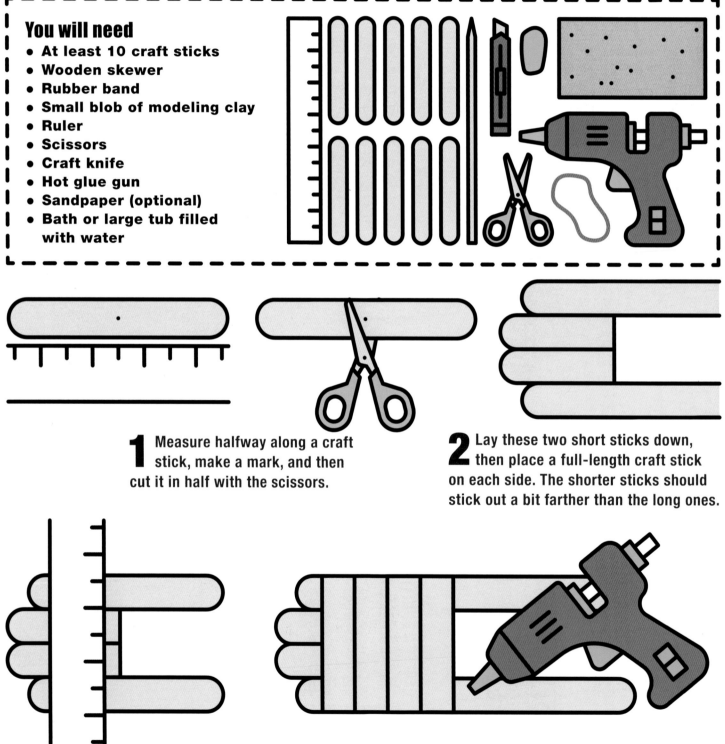

You will need
- At least 10 craft sticks
- Wooden skewer
- Rubber band
- Small blob of modeling clay
- Ruler
- Scissors
- Craft knife
- Hot glue gun
- Sandpaper (optional)
- Bath or large tub filled with water

1 Measure halfway along a craft stick, make a mark, and then cut it in half with the scissors.

2 Lay these two short sticks down, then place a full-length craft stick on each side. The shorter sticks should stick out a bit farther than the long ones.

3 Measure the width of the four sticks and make a note of it. Mark and cut six lengths of craft stick the same size.

4 Apply a line of glue across the first four sticks, near the end of the shorter sticks, and attach one of the short lengths you cut in step 3.

5 Glue three more of the sticks from step 3 across the deck of the boat.

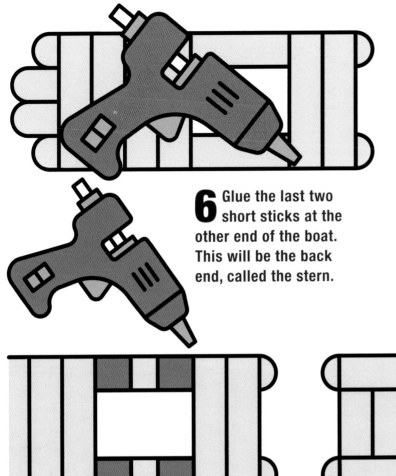

6 Glue the last two short sticks at the other end of the boat. This will be the back end, called the stern.

7 Cut four pieces of craft stick. They must be short enough for two of them to fit in the gap between the front and rear deck planks, leaving a small gap in between.

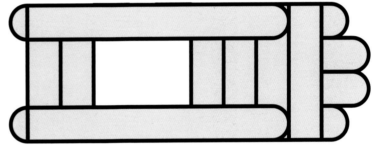

8 Glue them into place along each side, leaving a small gap for the rubber band.

9 Hold another craft stick so that the left hand end lines up with the second of the "deck planks" at the bow (front) of the boat. Cut off the other end where it sticks out over the stern.

10 Do the same on the other side and then glue both sticks into position.

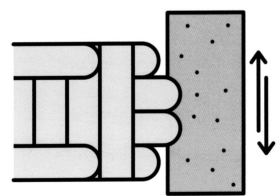

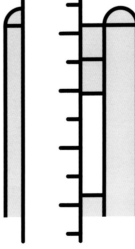

11 If you like, use sandpaper to shape and smooth the front of your boat. The boat will still work without sanding, but it will look nicer if you smooth out the rough edges.

12 Measure the length of the gap in your boat and cut two pieces of craft stick so that they're a little bit shorter than the gap. These pieces will form the paddle wheel, so they must be able to spin freely in that gap.

13 Ask an adult to line up the two bits of stick and use the craft knife to cut into them, halfway along. You need a notch in both sticks that runs about halfway through.

14 Slot two sticks together to form a cross. If you like, you can use sandpaper to round off the square ends of the paddles.

15 Thread the rubber band through the gap in your boat so it sticks out both sides.

16 Holding one end of the rubber band, loop the other end around the stern of the boat. Then do the same with the end of the rubber band. It will now be held in place.

17 Take the paddle wheel and slide one of the paddles between the two bits of rubber band. There should be enough tension to hold it in place.

In the real world

What you've actually built is a tiny paddle boat. In the 19th century, paddle boats steamed up and down the Mississippi River in the United States, ferrying hundreds of passengers at a time. These boats could be very luxurious, with ballrooms, bars, and fancy cabins.

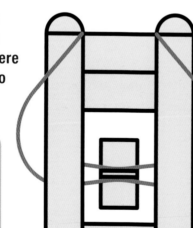

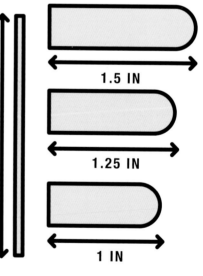

4.75 IN

1.5 IN

1.25 IN

1 IN

18 To make a mast and sail, cut three pieces of craft stick, one 1.5 inches (4 cm) long, one 1.25 inches (3.2 cm), and one 1 inch (2.5 cm). Cut a piece of skewer about 4.75 inches (12 cm) long.

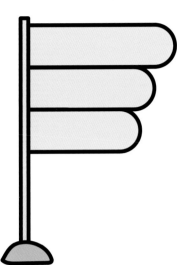

19 Line up the three craft stick pieces next to the skewer and glue them in place.

20 Use a small blob of modeling clay to attach the mast onto the deck of the boat.

Inside the engineering

When you wind the paddle, it twists the rubber band, which stores potential energy. When you release the paddle, the energy stored in the elastic is transferred to the paddle, making it turn. The paddle's "blades" spin, pushing water behind them and pushing the boat forward. It's also an example of Newton's Third Law of Motion.

21 Fill the bathtub with water, wind up the paddle (the more turns you can do, the farther the boat will go), and pop it into the water. Now watch it zoom away!

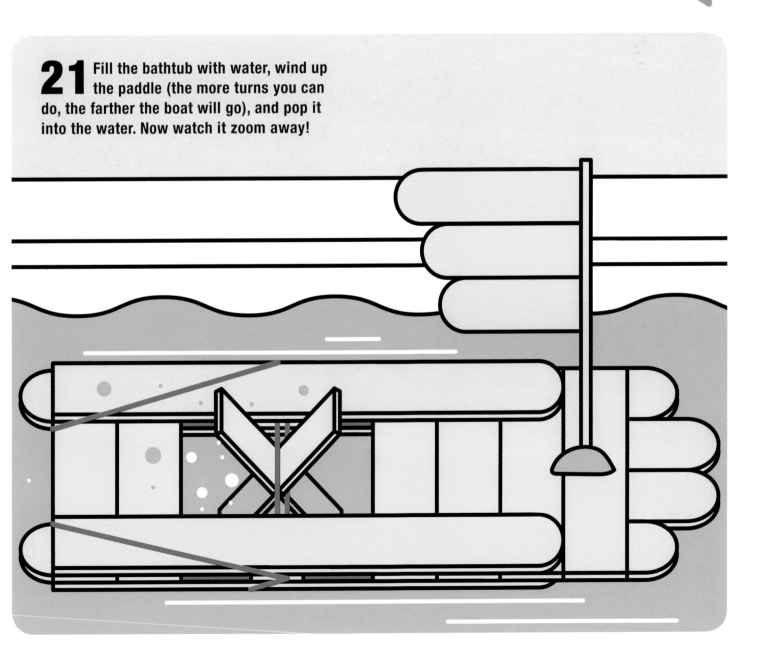

THE ELECTRIC LIGHT SHOW

There's a lot of light that is invisible to our eyes. But with the aid of the Electric Light Show, all is revealed!

1 Measure across the width of your box and find the middle. Then measure up about 1 inch (2.5 cm) from there and make a mark.

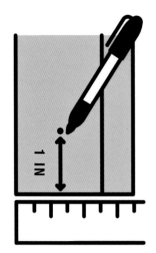

1 IN

You will need

- **Long, narrow rectangular cardboard box, or a big mailing tube**
- **Ruler**
- **Pen**
- **Electrical tape**
- **Scissors**
- **Coin**
- **Craft knife**
- **Protractor**
- **Old CD**

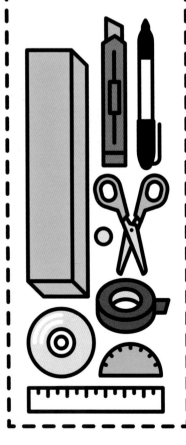

2 Put the coin over the dot and draw around it. Ask an adult to cut out the circle with the craft knife.

3 Turn the box around, so the hole you just made is on the right-hand side. Find the middle of this side of the box and make a dot that is level with the bottom of the hole you cut. Place the protractor with its center on that dot, then make another dot at the 60 degree mark.

4 Draw a line joining the two dots, then continue all the way up to the edge of the box.

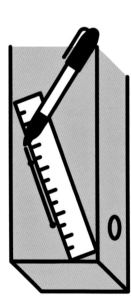

5 Repeat on the opposite side of the box and then join your two diagonal lines together across the back with a straight line.

6 Ask an adult to cut along the lines with the craft knife. Slide the CD into this slot, with the shiny side facing the hole you cut in step 2.

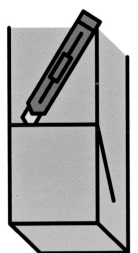

7 Open the other end of the box and cut off the lid.

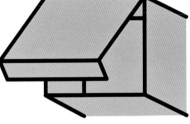

8 Stick strips of tape across the open end. You need to leave a little gap in the middle, running in the same direction as the straight line you made in step 5.

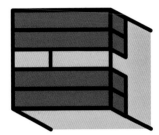

9 Add more tape running in the other direction, until you end up with just a small slit in the center.

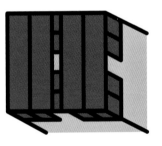

10 To use your light show, stand under a light and look through the eyehole to see a rainbow effect reflected on the CD.

WOW!

Inside the engineering

Depending on what you point it at, this device—called a spectroscope—will display a different light show. This is because different kinds of light have different properties. White light is a mixture of different colors—the colors that make up a rainbow. When white light is reflected by the grooves in the CD, the colors separate to form a **spectrum**. If you put your spectroscope under a light bulb the colors will fade into each other, while under a fluorescent light, the colors will be picked out very sharply. You can even take your spectroscope into daylight, as long as you avoid looking directly at the sun. Pointing your spectroscope toward a bright sky will give you strong black lines between the colors.

BALLOON RACER

You probably know that wind can power a boat, but can it move a car? Let's find out!

You will need
- **Small piece of thick cardboard**
- **Large empty matchbox or similar (for the body of the car)**
- **Two or three plastic straws**
- **Two wooden skewers**
- **Plastic bottle cap**
- **Balloon**
- **Strong tape**
- **Pen**
- **Scissors**

1 Cut two identical lengths of straw. They should each be just a bit narrower than the width of your matchbox.

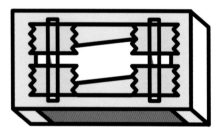

2 Tape the two straws into position, making sure to keep them as straight as possible.

3 Slide the wooden skewer through one of the straws. Make sure there's a bit of skewer sticking out on either side, then cut the stick.

4 Use the cut piece of skewer to measure off another identical piece, then cut it. These two bits of skewer will be your axles.

5 Put the bottle cap on the cardboard and draw around it four times. Cut out the four circles—these will be your wheels.

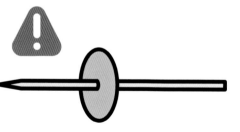

6 Use the sharp end of a skewer to poke a hole through the middle of each of the cardboard wheels.

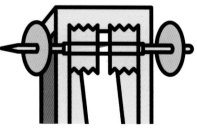

7 Slide one of the axles you made in step 4 through the front straw and push a cardboard wheel onto each end. Do the same with the back wheels.

8 Cut the end (the part you blow into) off the balloon, then slide the balloon over the end of a long straw and tape it tight. The better the seal, the farther your car will travel.

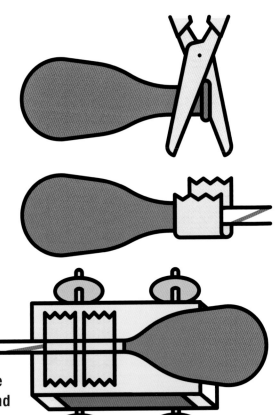

9 Tape the straw to the top of the car. The end where the balloon attaches should be roughly halfway along the body of the car.

Inside the engineering

When you blow up the balloon and cover the end, you are trapping air inside the balloon. The stretched elastic of the balloon has become an energy store. When you release the end of the straw the energy store is transferred to the trapped air, which rushes out the end. This is an example of Newton's third law of motion—for every action (air rushing out of the balloon) there must be an equal and opposite reaction (the car accelerating in the opposite direction).

10 Blow through the straw to inflate the balloon and cover the end with your finger. Place the car on a flat surface, uncover the end of the straw, and watch it go!

THE TREMBLING TOWER

Is it possible to build a tower out of skinny toothpicks that is sturdy enough to withstand an earthquake? Let's find out!

You will need

- **Wooden toothpicks or cocktail sticks**
- **Modeling dough**
- **Modeling clay**
- **A table**
- **A friend to help**

1/2 IN

1 Roll the modeling dough into a few small balls. They should each be about 1/2 inch (1.2 cm) across.

2 Make a square with four cocktail sticks and four of your dough balls.

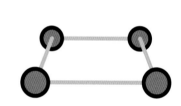

3 Add four more sticks, pointing up, to give your structure some height.

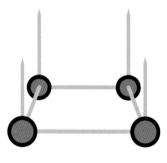

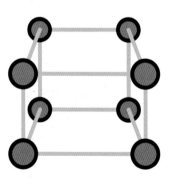

4 One at a time, add a ball of modeling dough to the top of each stick, connecting them with horizontal sticks as you go. You may need to get a bit of help from a friend.

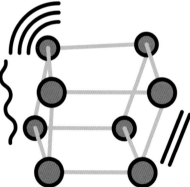

5 Make an "earthquake" by drumming the edge of the table with both hands so the top vibrates. Does your building stay upright?

In the real world

Buildings are designed to support loads from top to bottom—but earthquakes are dangerous because they shake them side to side. Engineers have tried different ways to make buildings earthquake-proof. Some are reinforced with steel, which bends and stretches to absorb shocks. Other buildings sit on top of ball bearings or springs, which help reduce the effect of the earthquake.

6 Fix your building, if necessary, then add four more cocktail sticks to make a second story.

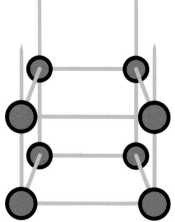

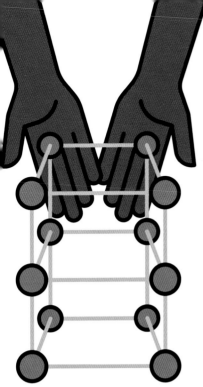

7 Add four more balls to the top, using horizontal cocktail sticks to connect them as you go. You'll definitely need a friend to help hold it!

Inside the engineering

Using a sticky material to join the cocktail sticks allows you to build a structure that is taller than if you just stacked the cocktail sticks up. However, although adding joints made of modeling dough lets you build higher, the dough is too soft to withstand an earthquake. The firmer, stickier modeling clay makes for a sturdier building.

8 Put your building in a safe place (not on the table). Repeat steps 1–7, but this time use the stiffer modeling clay rather than modeling dough.

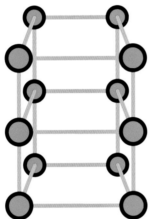

9 Put both buildings on the table and make another "earthquake" by drumming the table. The modeling-dough building will probably fall down. But modeling clay is firmer and stickier than the modeling dough, so that building should be able to stand up on its own and not be toppled by the "earthquake."

THE BOTTLE BLASTER

Want to make a plastic bottle fly through the air really, really fast? Try this bottle blaster!

You will need
- Two large plastic bottles, the same size
- Craft knife
- Scissors
- Duct tape
- Spool of elastic cord (the kind used in jewelry making)
- Measuring tape

1 Ask an adult to use the craft knife to make a cut in the first bottle, about a third of the way from the top. Then you can cut all the way around the bottle with the scissors.

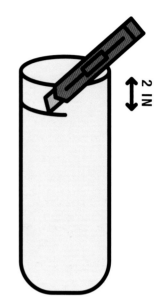
2 IN

2 Now you need to make the handles. Take the bottom section of the bottle, measure about 2 inches (5 cm) from the edge that you cut, and get your assistant to make another cut with the craft knife.

3 Cut around with the scissors and then cut the resulting circle in half again. You should end up with two loops that are each about 1 inch (2.5 cm) wide.

4 Cover any sharp edges by wrapping tape around your handles. Repeat steps 1–3 with the other bottle, so you have four handles covered with tape and two cut-off bottles.

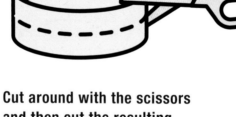

5 Push one of the cut-off bottle tops inside the other one and secure them with duct tape.

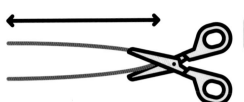

6 Measure out about 16.5 feet (5 m) of the elastic cord and then cut that in half.

8 Take the two free ends of cord and thread them all the way through the bottle blaster. Tie the ends to the two remaining handles.

7 Tie the end of one cord around one of the handles and make sure to knot it really tightly. Tie one end of the other cord to another handle in the same way.

Inside the engineering

This is an example of inertia—the tendency of an object to keep doing whatever it's doing. In this case, once the bottle blaster is moving, it will continue moving until something stops it. This could be either the other person's fingers or friction from the cord. Friction is the resistance that happens when one thing rubs against another.

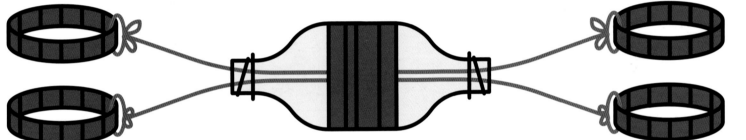

9 Get a friend to hold one set of handles while you hold the other. Stand far enough apart so that the cord is tight, with the bottle at your end of the cord. Quickly jerk your arms apart and the bottle will shoot down the line to your friend. When it does, close your arms and get your friend to open theirs—the bottle will shoot back to you.

BIG DIPPER

Cloudy night? No problem! Here's how to build your own "constellation," which you can enjoy whenever you like.

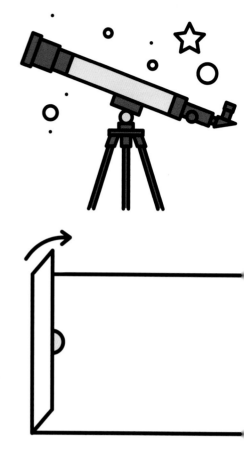

You will need

- **Sheet of printer paper**
- **Sheet of black cardstock**
- **Seven LED lights**
- **Copper tape**
- **3 volt round lithium ion battery**
- **Pen**
- **Pencil**
- **Ruler**
- **Small screwdriver**
- **Blob of modeling clay (optional)**

1 Place the printer paper sideways in front of you. Fold in the left hand edge enough to cover the width of the battery. Make a fold from the top to the bottom.

2 Measure in 1 inch (2.5 cm) from the edge of the folded paper and draw a small circle with your pencil. This is the first of your seven "stars."

1 IN

3 Draw six more "stars" and the connecting lines to complete your Big Dipper shape, using the image on the next page as a guide.

4 Use the pencil and ruler to draw a "frame" around the Big Dipper shape, about 1/2 inch (1.2 cm) from your line in each direction.

5 Place the battery on the lower end of the frame, with its left side touching the fold you made in step 1. Extend the top line of the frame over the battery, across the fold, and down the left side.

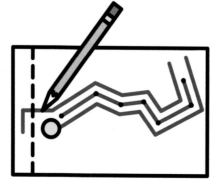

Here's an image of the Big Dipper shape.

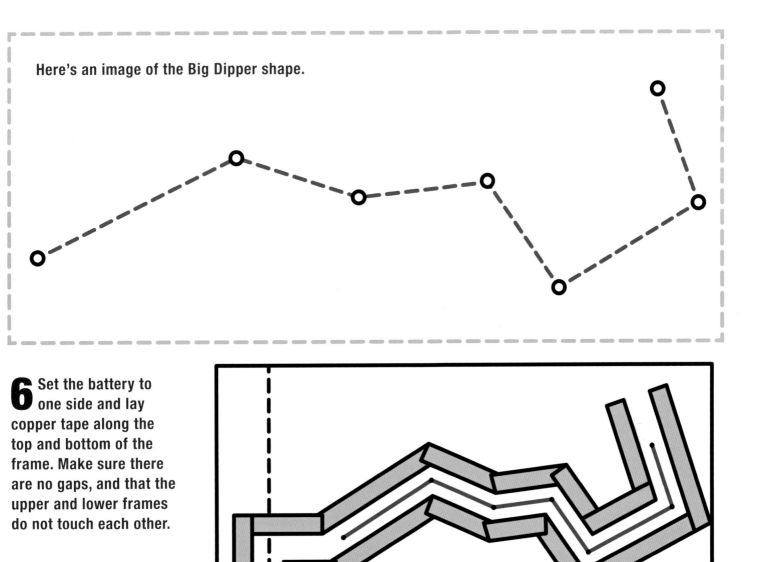

6 Set the battery to one side and lay copper tape along the top and bottom of the frame. Make sure there are no gaps, and that the upper and lower frames do not touch each other.

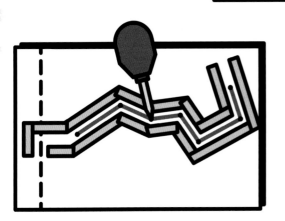

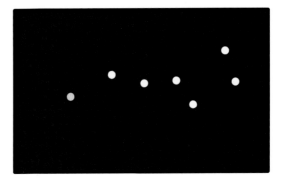

7 Place the sheet of black cardstock under the sheet you used for the Big Dipper and then carefully use the screwdriver to make holes under your seven "stars."

8 Widen the holes a bit and test them for size with one of the LED lights. They should be just big enough for the LED light to fit through. Set the black cardstock to one side.

9 Take one of the LEDs and bend both legs open. Place the longer leg on the top copper tape and the shorter one on the bottom, with the light over the first circle.

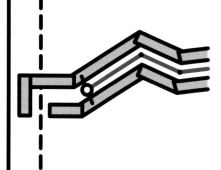

10 Place the battery on the end of the lower copper tape, making sure the "+" sign is facing up.

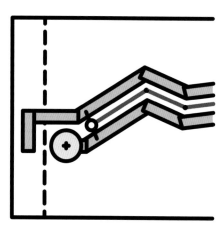

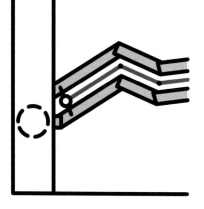

11 Fold the paper over the battery, so the end of the top run of copper tape touches the "+" side of the battery. The LED should light up.

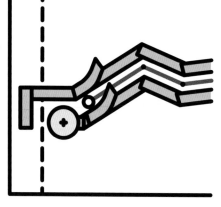

12 Position the LED over the circle as best you can and tape its legs down using tiny bits of copper tape.

13 Tape the other six LED lights over the other six circles in the same way. Make sure that the long leg is always touching the top line of copper tape, and the short leg is touching the bottom strip.

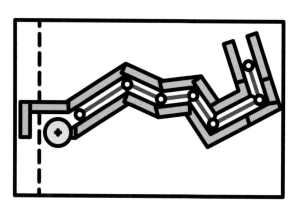

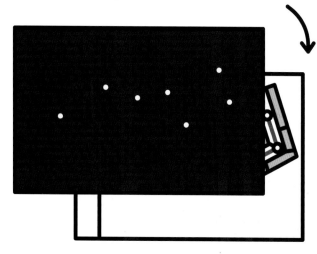

14 Slide the battery into position and fold the paper over it. Then place the black cardstock over the Big Dipper sheet.

Inside the engineering

The copper tape is really good at conducting electricity. By laying two parallel "tracks" and connecting the positive legs of the LEDs to the top one and the negative legs to the bottom one, you've created an electrical circuit. The circuit is completed when you press down on the paper so that the top copper strip touches the positive side of the battery and the bottom strip touches the negative side.

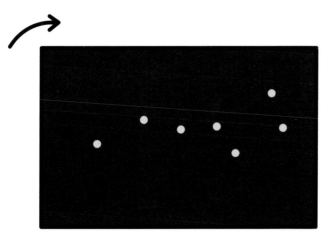

15 Carefully push the LED lights through the holes in the black paper.

Take it further To get the full effect of your constellation, try it in a room with the lights off! You can use adhesive putty to secure the cardstock and paper together at each corner. You could also use modeling clay to make a little "shelf" so you can slide the battery in and out when it's not in use.

16 Push down onto the black cardstock where the battery is to complete the circuit and your Big Dipper will appear. You may have to adjust the position of the battery slightly to make it work.

WOW!

THE WAVE MACHINE

Engineers and scientists talk about "waves" all the time. Light travels in waves, and so does sound. Why not build a machine that lets you see a wave moving backward and forward?

You will need
- 30 wooden skewers
- 60 mini marshmallows
- Duct tape
- Tape measure
- Ruler
- Scissors
- Two chairs or other pieces of furniture that are the same height

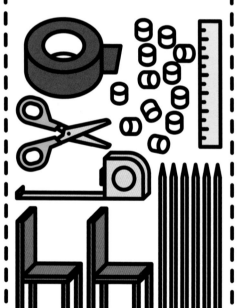

1 Use the sharp end of a skewer to poke a hole all the way through one of the marshmallows.

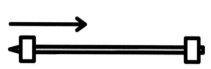

2 Pull the skewer out, turn it around, and insert the blunt end into the hole you just made. Put another marshmallow on the sharp end.

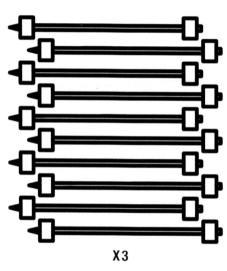

X3

3 Repeat steps 1 and 2 until you have 30 skewers, each with a marshmallow on both ends.

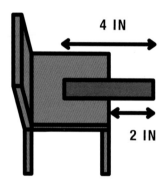

4 IN

2 IN

4 Measure and cut a 4 inch (10 cm) length of duct tape. Stick it onto the top of the first piece of furniture, with 2 inches (5 cm) of tape hanging over the edge.

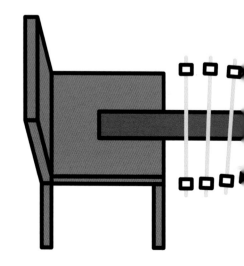

64 IN

5 Using the tape measure, place the second piece of furniture 64 inches (162 cm) from the first one. Stick a 4 inch (10 cm) length of tape to it, as you did in step 4.

7 Unroll the tape and cut a piece long enough to attach at the other chair. You should end up with a long, taut piece of tape. With the 2 inches (5 cm) of tape covering either end, you're left with 60 inches (152 cm) of visible sticky-side-up tape.

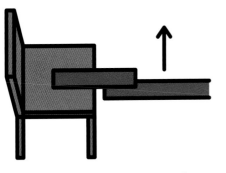

60 IN

6 Unwind some tape and stick it under the tape you attached to the first piece of furniture in step 4. The sticky side will be facing up.

Inside the engineering

Waves transfer energy— they are energy pathways. However, we cannot see sound or light waves. The wave machine models how a wave can transfer energy. When you tap, push, or lift one of the marshmallows, you transfer energy to it, which travels down the tape from one stick to the next. The marshmallows provide mass, which makes the skewers rotate more slowly. This makes the effect easier to see.

8 Center your first skewer on the tape, right where the sticky section starts. Add more skewers, 2 inches (5 cm) apart. Continue until you've attached all 30 skewers to the tape, lining them up straight.

Take it further Try using a heavier candy and see what difference it makes. You can also increase the length of the tape and the number of skewers to see if that changes what you see.

9 To see a wave, push down about 6 inches (15 cm) on a marshmallow at one end of the tape and then let go. You'll see a wave travel the length of the tape and then back again.

SMARTPHONE BOOMBOX

Love listening to music on your phone? Here's how to turbo-charge your sounds with a few household items.

You will need

- **Cardboard tube with plastic ends**
- **Ruler**
- **Marker**
- **Smartphone**
- **Craft knife**
- **Two paper cups**
- **Scissors**

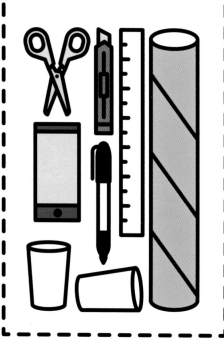

In the real world

Experiment by either using a larger tube or by adding bigger cups at the ends. You'll find that the more room the soundwaves have to bounce around, the louder they get.

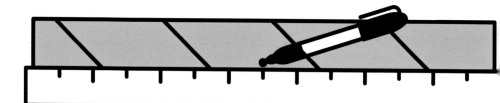

1 Start by taking the plastic ends off the cardboard tube. Next measure the length of the tube with a ruler and put a dot in the middle with your pen.

2 Then measure the width of your phone from edge to edge.

3 Place the center of the phone on the dot you made in step 2 and add two dots to mark the left and right edge of the phone.

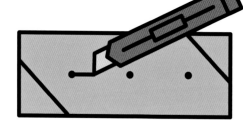

4 Get an adult to cut out a slot from the left dot to the right dot using the craft knife. Start with a narrow opening and keep widening it until your phone will fit snugly into the slot, but won't just drop all the way into it.

5 Now place one end of the tube onto the side of the first cup and draw a circle around it.

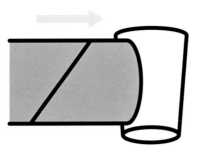

6 Use your scissors to cut around the circle to make a hole in the cup. Repeat steps 5 and 6 using the second cup.

7 Carefully push one end of the tube into the hole in the first plastic cup. Then do the same with the other cup.

Inside the engineering

Sound travels through the air as sound waves (vibrations in the air) that we can hear. Normally when the sound comes out of your phone, the vibrations spread out in all directions. Placing it inside the tube channels sound waves from the phone into the cups. The cups direct the sound waves toward you, making the sound louder and clearer.

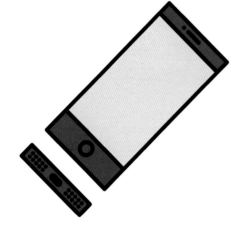

9 Start some music playing on your phone while holding it above the boombox. With the music still playing, push the phone into the slot, speaker end first. As you do, you'll notice that the music gets MUCH louder.

8 Make sure you know which end of your phone has the speaker.

BOOM!

BOOM!

THE SIMPLE MACHINES

The six simple machines are the screw, lever, inclined plane, pulley, wedge, and wheel and axle. What happens when you put them all together?

You will need
- **Cardboard (larger than printer size)**
- **Books to stack up**
- **Two screws**
- **Masking tape**
- **Length of foam pipe insulation, halved down the middle**
- **Glasses case with curved sides**
- **Paper towel tube**
- **Wooden skewer**
- **Two marbles**
- **Two small plastic cups (the type used for taking medicine)**
- **Ruler, 6 inches (15 cm) long**
- **Modeling clay or adhesive putty**
- **Empty thread spool**
- **Cotton thread**
- **Matchstick**
- **Scissors**
- **Balloon**
- **Toy car**
- **Pin**
- **Ring binder**
- **Table**

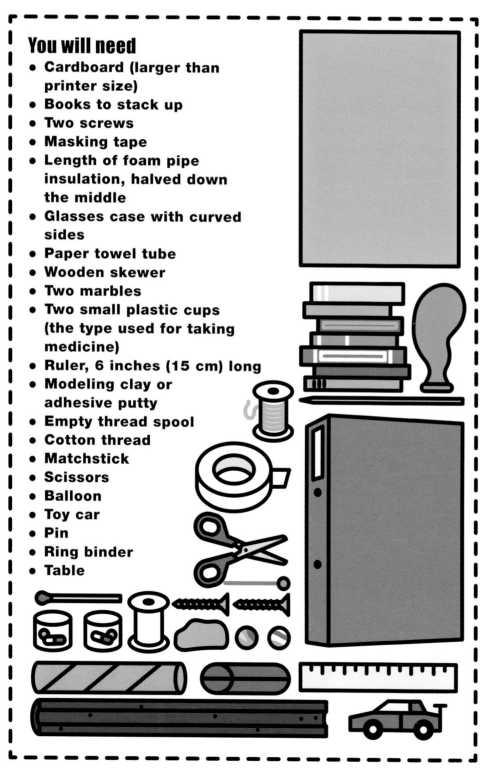

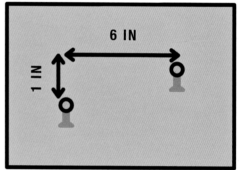

2.75 IN · 1 IN

1 Cut a piece of cardboard about the size of a piece of printer paper and push a screw into it. The screw should be 1 inch (2.5 cm) in from the shorter side and about 2.75 inches (7 cm) down the longer side.

6 IN · 1 IN

2 Put a second screw into the cardboard about 6 inches (15 cm) to the left of the first one, and about 1 inch (2.5 cm) lower.

3 Cut out a strip of cardboard. It should be just shorter than the length of a piece of printer paper and about one and a half times wider than the marbles.

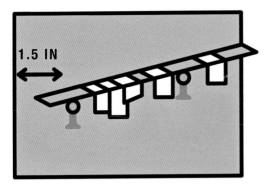

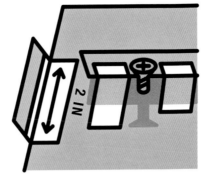

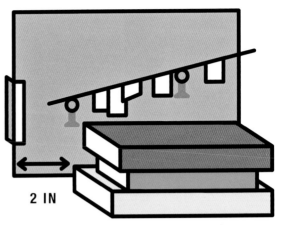

2 IN

4 Lay the cardboard strip on top of the two screws to create a ramp and tape it in place. Make sure you leave a gap of about 1.5 inches (4 cm) between the lower end of the ramp and the edge of the cardboard.

5 Cut a short piece of cardboard about 2 inches (5 cm) long and tape it to the edge of the cardboard near the bottom of the ramp. It will act as a "stop" to prevent the marble from flying off.

6 Make two piles of books. Slide your sheet of cardboard between the piles, so it stands up. It should stick out from the edge by 2 inches (5 cm) or so.

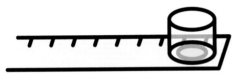

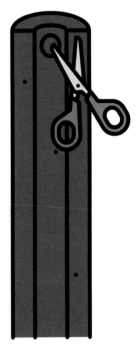

7 Attach one of the plastic medicine cups to the end of the ruler with a bit of modeling clay or adhesive putty.

8 Place the glasses case on top of a short stack of books or a small cardboard box. Balance the ruler-and-cup on top of the glasses case. (If you don't have a curved glasses case, try a spice jar, empty toilet paper tube, or even a banana!) The cup should sit below the end of the ramp.

9 Use scissors to cut a tiny notch or dip at one end of the pipe insulation.

10 Place the notched end of the pipe on top of another pile of books so that it sticks out over the top of the empty end of the ruler.

11 Use the skewer to poke a hole all the way through one end of the paper towel tube.

3 FT

12 Cut a piece of thread a little over 3 feet (about 1 m) long and tie one end around the matchstick. Tape the other end to the other medicine cup.

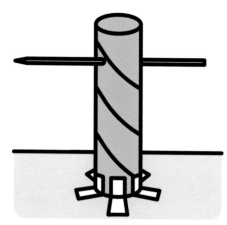

13 Tape the paper towel tube to the edge of the table next to the lower end of the ramp from step 10. The wooden skewer should be parallel with the table's edge.

14 Wrap the middle part of the thread around the thread spool and then slide that onto the skewer. Place the medicine cup at the bottom of the ramp, ready to catch the marble.

15 Measure the ring binder and cut two strips of cardboard that are as long as its cover is wide. Tape these strips down on the binder to make a "track" that will keep your toy car rolling in a straight line.

17 Place the ring binder next to the paper towel tube, with the taller side along the table's edge.

16 Attach the pin to the front of the car using modeling clay or adhesive putty. Angle the pin so that it is pointing slightly up.

POP!

Inside the engineering

The marble rolls down the ramp and drops into the cup. This raises the other end of the ruler, which knocks into the pipe insulation ramp, setting the second marble in motion. That marble hits the other cup and pushes it off the ramp, pulling down on the thread. The thread pulls the matchstick out and the binder closes, so the car rolls down the slope and the pin pops the balloon. Have you spotted the six simple machines? Screws in the cardboard support the first ramp. The ruler on the glasses case forms a lever, and the pipe insulation is an inclined plane. The thread spool and thread make a pulley. The car's wheels and axles allow it to roll. The pointed end of the pin is a wedge, which pushes into the balloon.

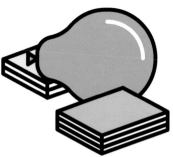

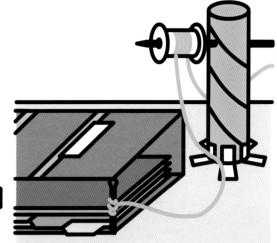

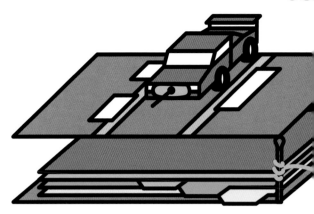

18 Blow up the balloon and place it in line with where the car will roll down off the binder. Use two books to hold it in place.

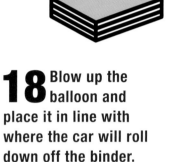

19 Lift the cover of the binder and use the match to prop it open. The match should be in the front corner, nearest to the paper towel tube. The thread between the match and the thread spool shouldn't be too loose or too tight.

20 Place the car on the ring binder, between the tracks.

21 Everything is now in place and you're ready to go. Start by placing a marble at the top of the ramp you made in steps 1–5. Then let it go and watch what happens!

GLOSSARY

Not sure of the meaning of a particular engineering term or phrase? Well, you've come to the right place—let's remind ourselves what all these words actually mean!

aerodynamic designed in such a way that it offers the least possible resistance to the air

alternating current type of electricity used in homes, in which the current changes direction many times a second

amplify to increase the volume of a sound to make it louder, such as by cupping your hands around your mouth

axle rod that goes through the center of a wheel, forming one of the six simple machines. Axles may be fixed so the wheel spins, or actually spin themselves with the wheel.

buoyancy force which makes things float on water or another fluid

charge property of matter that can be either positive or negative

circuit path followed by electricity in an electronic device. Circuits are usually made up of wires.

compression the force that pushes inward on something such as a joint in a structure

conductor substance which can easily transmit electricity or heat

direct current type of electricity supplied by batteries, in which the current flows in one direction

drag slowing force that pushes against an object as it moves through air or water

energy ability to do work or make things happen

equilateral having all sides the same length

force a push or a pull

friction resistance force that occurs when one thing rubs against another thing

geodesic the shortest path between two points on a curved surface

gravity force that attracts an object toward any other object having mass

homopolar motor type of simple motor that works with a direct electrical current

inclined plane ramp or slope that is one of the six simple machines

inertia tendency of something to either stay still or keep moving in a straight line

keystone a central stone that fits into the very top of an arch and fixes it in place

kinetic energy a moving object's energy store

LED ("light emitting diode") type of semiconductor which gives off light when electricity is passed through it

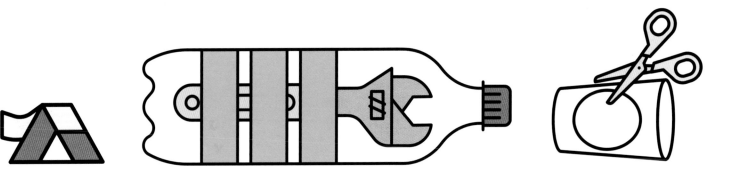

lever bar that rests on a pivot (central point) like a seesaw. Levers are one of the six simple machines.

magnetic field a region around a magnet than can attract magnetic materials and repel other magnets

Magnus effect a force that acts on a spinning object that causes it to swerve upward, downward, or sideways

mass amount of matter that an object contains. Mass is often measured in pounds and ounces, but it is not quite the same as weight.

momentum the mass of an object multiplied by its velocity

neodymium type of magnet up to 100 times stronger than a "normal" magnet

Newton's Laws of Motion three laws defined by Isaac Newton in the 1600s. They formed the basis for all mechanical engineering.

pentagon two-dimensional shape with five sides

potential energy energy stored by an object that is stretched, twisted, bent, squashed, or high up

pressure force acting over an area

pulley a wheel and cord arranged so that pulling down on one end of the cord pulls up whatever is on the other end. One of the six simple machines.

screw simple machine that converts motion going around and around into motion that goes forward

simple machine one of six essential machines which form the basis for many other, more complex machines

tension state of being pulled on and stretched tight

vibration very quick back-and-forth movement. Drumming your hands on the top of a table will create vibrations.

visible spectrum colors of light that make up a rainbow that we can see with our eyes

wedge triangular shape used to separate two objects or to fix something in place. Wedges are one of the six simple machines.

wheel rotating disc which usually spins around an axle, forming one of the six simple machines

INDEX

adult supervision 5, 7
aerodynamic 63
air pressure 43, 53
alternating current 25
arches 68–69

Balloon Racer 76–77
batteries 6
Big Dipper 82–85
Bottle Blaster 80–81
Bottle Rocket 56–57
Bottle Sub 66–67
Bouncing Bridge 34–37
buoyancy 67

carbon dioxide 57
catapults 16–17
Clothesline Flyer 46–49
compression 27
conservation of energy 13
conservation of momentum 13
copper tape 6
copper wire 6
craft knife 6
craft sticks 6
Crafty Catapult 16–17
crocodile clips 6

Dancing Robot 64–65
domes 26–27
Double Cup Flyer 42–43
duct tape 7

earthquakes 37, 78
Electric Light Show 74–75
Electric Spinner 50–51
electrical circuits 14–15, 31,
    51, 84
electricity 14, 25, 31, 51, 84
energy transfer 17, 45, 63, 65,
    73, 77, 87
Engineer's Arm 32–33

equipment 6–7

flyers 42–43, 46–49, 62–63,
    80–81
friction 81

Geodesic Dome 26–27
graphite 31
gravity 29

Hanging Arch 68–69
Hexbug 7
Hi-Tech Hand 20–21
hinges 33
Homemade Nightlight 30–31
homopolar motor 51
hot glue gun 7

inertia 29, 65, 81

Jumping Marbles 28–29

keystones 69
kinetic energy 17, 63

LEDs 7
levers 90, 92
light bulbs 30–31
light waves 86, 87
loudspeakers 22–25

Magnetic Spinner 40–41
magnets 7, 65
Magnus effect 43
Marble Maze 58–61
Marble Roller Coaster 44–45
masking tape 7
momentum 13

neodymium magnets 7
Newton's Cradle 10–13
Newton's Third Law of Motion
    57, 73, 77

paddle boats 70–73
Paper Loudspeaker 22–25
Paper Pillars 8–9
Paper Popper 52–53
pillars 8–9
pipe insulation 7
potential energy 63, 73
protractor 7
pulleys 21, 90, 92
pyramids 18

ramps (inclined planes) 60,
    90, 92
ring magnets 7
Robot Artist 54–55
robots 20–21, 54–55, 64–65
rockets 56–57, 62–63
Rubber Band Boat 70–73

screws 49, 90, 92
Simple Circuit 14–15
simple machines 39, 60, 90–93
Smartphone Boombox 88–89
sound waves 86, 87, 88, 89
spectroscope 74–75
spinners 40–43, 50–51, 64–65
submarines 66–67
Supersonic Straw 62–63
suspension bridges 34–37

thrust 49
Tower of Triangles 18–19
Trembling Tower 78–79
triangles 18–19, 27

Wave Machine 86–87
Weather Vane 38–39
wedges 90, 92
wheel and axle 39, 90, 92
white light 75